W9-AVL-480

Gold Stars

KINDERGARTEN
BIG WORKBOOK

PaRragon.

This edition published by Cottage Door Press, LLC, in 2019.
First published 2017 by Parragon Books, Ltd.

Copyright © 2019 Cottage Door Press, LLC
5005 Newport Drive, Rolling Meadows, Illinois 60008

Written by Nina Filipek and Catherine Casey
Cover Art by Abi Hall
Illustrated by Simon Abbott and Adam Linley
Educational Consultant: Marla Conn, Read-Ability, Inc.

ISBN: 978-1-68052-692-9

Printed in China

Gold Stars™ is an imprint of Cottage Door Press, LLC.
Parragon Books® and the Parragon® logo are registered trademarks of Cottage Door Press, LLC.

Contents

Writing

Helping Your Child

- Remember, the writing activities in this book should be enjoyed by your child. Always stop before your child grows tired.

- Try to find a quiet place to work with plenty of space and a hard surface.

- By working through these activities, your child will begin to control a pencil or pen and move on to letter formation.

- Show your child how you hold a pencil or pen. It doesn't matter which hand they use to write with at this stage.

- This book uses standard letter formation. Some schools use a slightly different handwriting policy. Check with your child's teacher.

- Always give your child lots of encouragement and praise.

Contents

The Alphabet

Connect the dotted lines to write each letter of the alphabet. Use different colors to make a pattern.

Note for parent: This activity gives your child practice in writing all the lowercase (small) letters of the alphabet. Have fun trying to think of a word that begins with each letter.

 m m m m

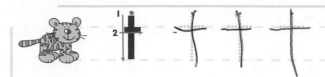 t t t t

 n n n n

 u u u u

 o o o o

 v v v v

 p p p p

 w w w w

 q q q q

 x x x x

 r r r r

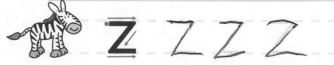 y y y y

 s s s s

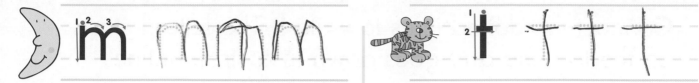 z z z z

Writing Letter l

Connect the dotted lines to write l. The letter l starts on the top line and goes down in a straight line.

Write the letter l to finish the words.

adybug   adybug

amb amb amb

eaf eaf eaf eaf

Write the letter l on your own.

Writing Letter t

Connect the dotted lines to write **t**. The letter **t** goes straight down. Then add a bar across.

Write the letter **t** to finish the words.

tent tent tent

rain rain rain

tree tree tree

Write the letter **t** on your own.

Writing Letter i

Connect the dotted lines to write **i**. The letter **i** goes down in a straight line. Then add a dot above.

Write the letter **i** to finish the words.

ice cream ice cream

igloo igloo igloo

iron iron iron

Write the letter **i** on your own.

Writing Letter j

Connect the dotted lines to write **j**. The letter **j** goes down, then curves left. Then add a dot on top.

j ⋮ ⋮ ⋮ ⋮ ⋮ ⋮ ⋮ ⋮ ⋮ ⋮ ⋮ ⋮ ⋮ j

Write the letter **j** to finish the words.

am　am　am　am

 ug　ug　ug　ug

igsaw　igsaw

Write the letter **j** on your own.

Writing Letter u

Connect the dotted lines to write **u**. The letter **u** goes down, around, up, and then down again.

u u u u u u u u u u

Write the letter **u** to complete the words.

umbrella umbrella

 up up up up up

under under under

Write the letter **u** on your own.

Note for parent: The letters u and y are formed in a similar way except that y has a tail.

Connect the dotted lines to write **y**. The letter **y** goes down, up, and then down in a diagonal line.

y   y   y   y   y   y   y   y

Write the letter **y** to complete the words.

yo-yo   yo-yo   yo-yo

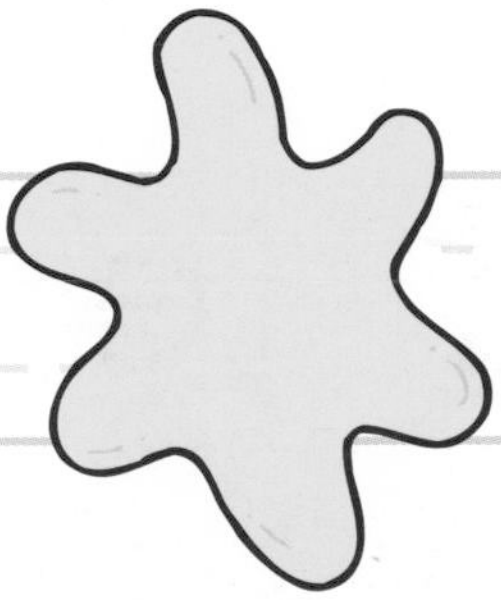

yellow   yellow

yum   yum   yum

Write the letter **y** on your own.

Writing Letter r

Connect the dotted lines to write **r**. The letter **r** goes down, then up again and over.

 r r r r r r r r r r

Write the letter **r** to finish the words.

robot robot robot

 red red red red

ring ring ring ring

Write the letter **r** on your own.

Note for parent: This activity focuses on the formation of the letters r and n. You can point out the similarities in how they are formed.

Writing Letter n

Connect the dotted lines to write **n**. The letter **n** goes down, then up again, then bends back down.

Write the letter **n** to finish the words.

nest   nest   nest

net   net   net   net

name   name   name

Anna

Write the letter **n** on your own.

Writing Letter m

Connect the dotted lines to write **m**. The letter **m** goes down, up and over, then up and over again.

Write the letter **m** to finish the words.

Write the letter **m** on your own.

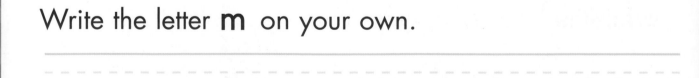

Note for parent: The letters m, h, and k are formed in a similar way.

Writing Letters h and k

Connect the dotted lines to write **h**. The letter **h** goes down, up halfway, then bends back down.

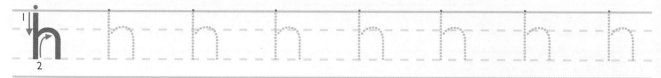

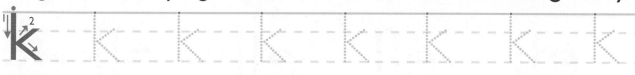

Write the letter **h** on your own.

Write letter **k**. Go down, up halfway, then do a diagonal line up, go back down, and kick out diagonally.

Write the letter **k** on your own.

Connect the dotted lines to write **b**. The letter **b** goes down, halfway up, then around to join at the bottom.

b b b b b b b b b

Write the letter **b** to finish the words.

bed bed bed

 bee bee bee bee

bell bell bell bell

Write the letter **b** on your own.

Note for parent: These two pages focus on the formation of the letters b and p—their similarities and differences.

Writing Letter p

Connect the dotted lines to write **p**. The letter **p** goes down to make a tail, then up, then curves around.

Write the letter **p** to finish the words.

panda panda

 pen pen pen pen

pear pear pear

Write the letter **p** on your own.

Writing Letters c and e

Connect the dotted lines to write **c**. The letter **c** goes down and around.

c c c c c c c c c c c c

car car car

Write the letter **c** on your own.

Connect the dotted lines to write **e**. The letter **e** starts in the middle, curves up, then goes halfway around.

e e e e e e e e e e e e

egg egg egg

Write the letter **e** on your own.

Note for parent: Encourage your child to try to make the letters c and e the same size.

Writing Letter a

Connect the dotted lines to write **a**. The letter **a** goes down, around, and back down again.

Write the letter **a** to finish the words.

pple pple pple

nt nt nt nt

rrow rrow rrow

Write the letter **a** on your own.

Note for parent: Show your child how the a joins at the top and then comes back down to the line.

21

Writing Letter d

Connect the dotted lines to write **d**. The letter **d** goes down, around, up to the top, and then back down.

 d d d d d d d d

Write the letter **d** to finish the words.

og og og og

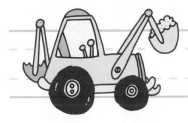 igger igger

uck uck uck

Write the letter **d** on your own.

Note for parent: Show your child how the letters a and d are similar.

Writing Letter o

Connect the dotted lines to write **o**. The letter **o** goes around to the left and joins up at the start.

O o o o o o o o o

Write the letter **o** to finish the words.

orange orange

open open open

owl owl owl owl

Write the letter **o** on your own.

Note for parent: The letters o, a, and d are all counterclockwise letters.

23

Writing Letter g

Connect the dotted lines to write **g**. The letter **g** goes down, around, then down with the tail curling left.

g g g g g g g g g g

Write the letter **g** to finish the words.

gate gate gate

 goat goat goat

girl girl girl girl

Write the letter **g** on your own.

Note for parent: This activity groups g and q together because they have a similar formation, except that the tails go in different directions.

Writing Letter q

Connect the dotted lines to write **q**. The letter **q** goes around, then down with the tail flicking right.

 q q q q q q q q

Write the letter **q** to finish the words.

quack quack

queen queen

quilt quilt quilt

Write the letter **q** on your own.

Writing Letter s

Connect the dotted lines to write **s**. The letter **s** curves backward, then curves forward.

S s s s s s s s s

Write the letter **s** to finish the words.

snake snake

 socks socks

sun sun sun sun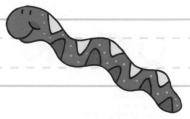

Write the letter **s** on your own.

Note for parent: The letter s is tricky because it turns both counterclockwise and clockwise.

Writing Letter f

Connect the lines to write **f**. The letter **f** curves down to make a tail, then finishes with a bar across.

f f f f f f f f f f f

Write the letter **f** to finish the words.

ish ish ish ish

flower flower

flag flag flag

Write the letter **f** on your own.

Writing Letter v

Connect the dotted lines to write **v**. The letter **v** goes diagonally down, then diagonally up, making a sharp point.

Write the letter **v** to finish the words.

van van van van

 ase ase ase

violin violin

Write the letter **v** on your own.

Note for parent: Show your child the sharp points at the bottom of the v and w.

Writing Letter w

Connect the dotted lines to write **w**. The letter **w** goes diagonally down, then up, then down, then up again!

w w w w w w w w w w

Write the letter **w** to finish the words.

witch witch witch

wand wand wand

wall wall wall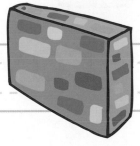

Write the letter **w** on your own.

Writing Letter x

Connect the dotted lines to write **x**. The letter **x** goes diagonally down to the right, then down to the left.

Write the letter **x** to finish the words.

fo× fo× fo× fo×

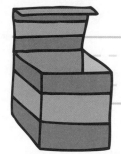

bo× bo× bo× bo×

×-ray ×-ray ×-ray

Write the letter **x** on your own.

Note for parent: Discuss with your child how their pencil must be lifted off the page to write x.

Connect the dotted lines to write **z**. The letter **z** goes across, then down to the left, then across again.

z z z z z z z z z z

Write the letter **z** to finish the words.

zebra zebra

zipper zipper

buzz buzz buzz

Write the letter **z** on your own.

Note for parent: Compare the letter z with the letter s on page 26 and talk about the differences.

31

Writing c, o, and a

Trace the letters with your finger. Then connect the dotted lines to write the letters. Start at the red dot and follow the arrow.

cat

The letter **C** goes down and around.

c c c c c c c

cake

car

Note for parent: The letters in this activity all begin at the top and move down in a counterclockwise direction.

The letter **O** goes down, around, and joins up at the start.

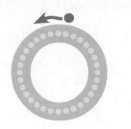

orange

owl

The letter **a** goes down, around, and back down again.

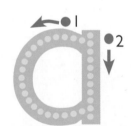

ant

apple

Writing d, g, and q

Trace the letters with your finger. Then connect the dotted lines to write the letters. Start at the red dot.

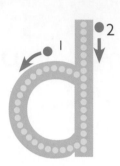

dog

The letter **d** goes down, around, up to the top, and back down.

duck

Note for parent: These letters give practice in adding upward and downward strokes. Show your child how the tails on the g and q are different.

The letter **g** goes down, around, and down below the line with a curly tail.

girl

gate

The letter **q** goes down, around, and below the line with a tick at the end of its tail.

queen

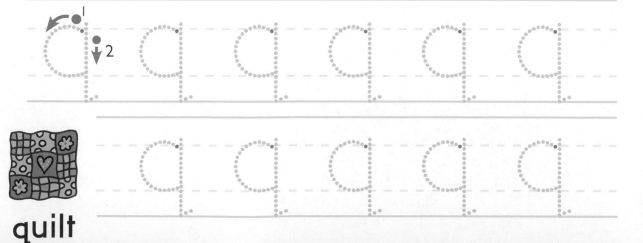

quilt

Writing r, n, m, and h

Trace the letters with your finger. Then connect the dotted lines to write the letters. Start at the red dot.

The letter **r** goes down, up, and over.

rat

r r r r r r

ring

r r r r r r

The letter **n** goes down, up and around, then back down.

net

n n n n n n

n n n n n n

nut

Note for parent: The letters in this activity all begin with a straight line. Show your child that the h is taller than the n.

The letter **m** goes down, up and around, then up and around again.

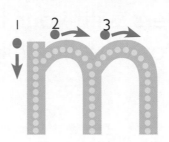

mug

mop

The letter **h** goes down, up halfway, around, and down again.

hen

house

Writing b, p, and k

Trace the letters with your finger. Then connect the dotted lines to write the letters. Start at the red dot.

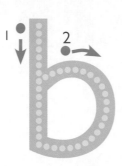

The letter **b** goes down, up halfway and around to join at the bottom.

boy

box

ball

Note for parent: The letters in this activity trace back up to the middle of the stroke.

The letter **p** goes down to make a tail, up to the top and around to join halfway down.

pig

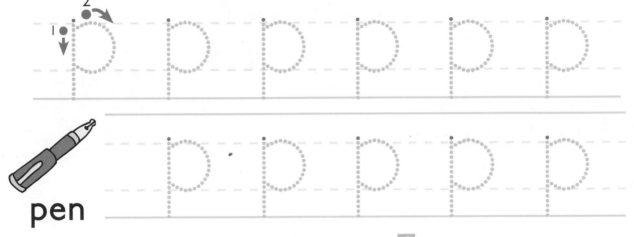

pen

The letter **k** goes down, up halfway, up diagonally, back down then kicks out.

key

kite

39

Writing l, i, and j

Trace the letters with your finger. Then connect the dotted lines to write the letters. Start at the red dot.

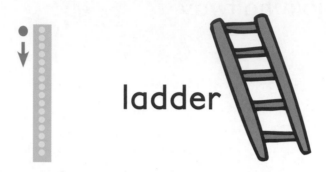

ladder

The letter **l** goes down.

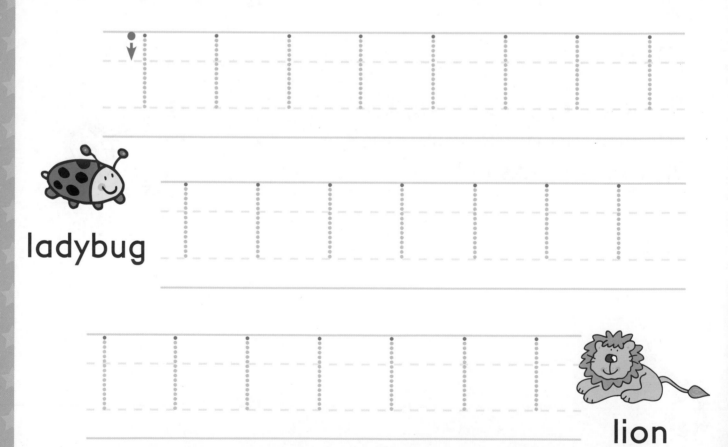

ladybug

lion

The letter **i** goes down, then add a dot above.

igloo

in

The letter **j** goes down and curves left. Then add a dot above.

jar

jam

Writing t, u, and y

Trace the letters with your finger. Then connect the dotted lines to write the letters. Start at the red dot.

tent

The letter **t** goes down and has a bar across.

teddy

tractor

Note for parent: Show your child how the bar crosses the down stroke.

The letter **u** goes down, around, up, and then down.

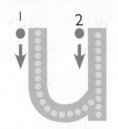

umbrella

up

The letter **y** goes down, up, and then down in a diagonal line.

yo-yo

yellow

Note for parent: Try tracing letters in the air with your child.

43

Writing v, w, x, and z

Trace the letters with your finger. Then connect the dotted lines to write the letters. Start at the red dot.

The letter **V** goes down and up, making a sharp point.

van

v v v v v v v

vegetables

V V V V V V V

The letter **W** goes down, up, down and up, making two sharp points.

web

w w w w w w w

witch

W W W W W W W

Note for parent: These letters are all zigzag shapes so it is helpful to practice them together.

The letter **X** goes down to the right, then down to the left.

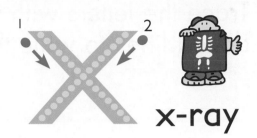

x-ray

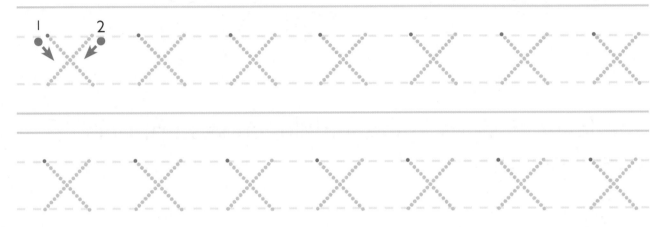

The letter **Z** goes across, down to the left then across again.

zebra

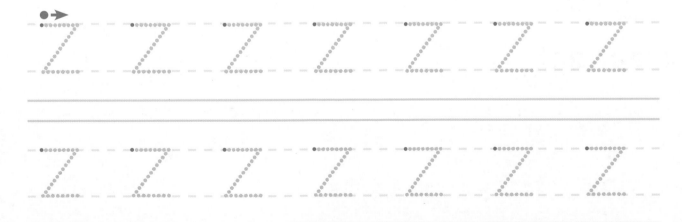

Writing e, f, and s

Trace the letters with your finger. Then connect the dotted lines to write the letters. Start at the red dot.

egg

The letter **e** starts in the middle, curves up, and goes halfway around.

elephant

Note for parent: These letters can be tricky but practice will help your child gain confidence.

The letter **f** curves down to make a tail, then finishes with a bar across.

fox

f f f f f f f f f

fish

f f f f f f f f

The letter **S** curves backward then curves forward.

sun

s s s s s s s s s

snake

s s s s s s s s

Writing Capitals A and B

Connect the dotted lines to write the capital letters. Capital letters are used at the start of names and the start of sentences.

I'm Ava.

A goes down diagonally from the top in different directions, then a bar goes across.

A A A A A A A A

Write the capital letter **A** on your own.

B goes down, then up, curves around to the middle, then around again.

B B B B B B

I'm Ben.

Write the capital letter **B** on your own.

Note for parent: This activity shows your child how to write and use a capital letter when writing a person's name.

Writing Capitals C and D

Connect the dotted lines to write the capital letters.

I'm Cara.

C goes halfway around.

Write the capital letter C on your own.

D goes down, then back to the top, then curves down to the line.

I'm Daisy.

Write the capital letter D on your own.

Writing Capitals E and F

Connect the dotted lines to write the capital letters.

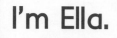

E goes down first, then across, across, across.

Write the capital letter **E** on your own.

F goes down first, then across, across.

Write the capital letter **F** on your own.

Note for parent: This activity shows your child how to write more capital letters with bars across.

Writing Capitals G and H

Connect the dotted lines to write the capital letters.

G curves around, then up halfway to finish with a bar across.

G   G   G   G   G   G

Write the capital letter **G** on your own.

H goes down, down again, then across the middle.

I'm Harry.

Write the capital letter **H** on your own.

Writing Capitals I and J

Connect the dotted lines to write the capital letters.

I goes down then across the top and bottom.

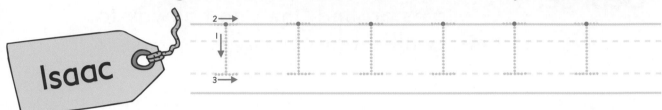

Write the capital letter I on your own.

J goes down and curls, then across at the top.

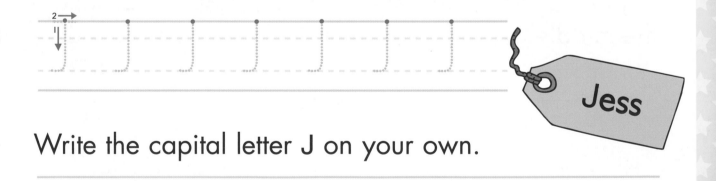

Write the capital letter J on your own.

Connect the dotted lines to write the capital letters.

K goes down, then diagonally to the middle before kicking out.

Katie

Write the capital letter **K** on your own.

L goes down, then across.

Luke

Write the capital letter **L** on your own.

Writing Capitals M and N

Capital letters are also used at the beginning of place names. Connect the dotted lines to write the capital letters.

Maine

M goes down, then up, then diagonally down, diagonally up, then down again.

Write the capital letter **M** on your own.

N goes down, then up, then diagonally down, then up again.

Nevada

Write the capital letter **N** on your own.

Note for parent: This activity reinforces how capital letters are used for place names.

Writing Capitals O and P

Connect the dotted lines to write the capital letters.

O goes around counterclockwise.

Ohio

O O O O O O

Write the capital letter O on your own.

P goes down, then up, then curves around
to the middle.

P P P P P P P

Portland

Write the capital letter P on your own.

Writing Capitals Q and R

Connect the dotted lines to write the capital letters. Then complete the road names.

Q goes around, then finishes with a diagonal bar.

Q Q Q Q Q

_ueens Drive

Write the capital letter **Q** on your own.

R goes down, up, then curves around to the middle and kicks out.

R R R R R R

_eno _oad

Write the capital letter **R** on your own.

Note for parent: This activity shows your child how to use capital letters for road names.

Connect the dotted lines to write the capital letters. Then complete the dinosaur names.

S curves backward then curves forward.

S S S S S S

_tegosaurus

Write the capital letter **S** on your own.

T goes down then across the top.

2 → T T T T
1 ↓

_elmatosaurus

Write the capital letter **T** on your own.

Note for parent: Encourage your child to try reading the dinosaur names.

57

Writing Capitals U and V

Connect the dotted lines to write the capital letters. Then complete the dinosaur names.

U goes down then up.

U U U U U

_ltrasaurus

Write the capital letter **U** on your own.

V goes diagonally down, then up.

V V V V V

Draw your own dinosaur here and give it a name beginning with **V**.

Write the capital letter **V** on your own.

Writing Capitals W and X

Connect the dotted lines to write the capital letters.
Then write capital letters to complete the signs.
W goes diagonally down, then
diagonally up (twice)!

W W W W W

_ARNING!

Write the capital letter **W** on your own.

NO
E_IT

X goes diagonally down
in different directions.

X X X X X

Write the capital letter **X** on your own.

Note for parent: Remind your child that the pencil is lifted to complete the letter X .

59

Writing Capitals Y and Z

Connect the dotted lines to write the capital letters. Then write capital letters to complete the signs.

Y goes diagonally down to the middle, then diagonally down the other way.

_ IELD

Write the capital letter **Y** on your own.

Z goes across, then diagonally down, then across again.

DANGER
_ONE

Write the capital letter **Z** on your own.

Note for parent: Capital Y and Z are double the height of a lowercase letter. Use the line at the top as a guide.

Capital Letters

Here are the capital letters together. They are used for people's names and the names of countries, towns, rivers, days and months, and much more.

Connect the dotted lines in the capital letters. Start at the red dot and follow the arrows.

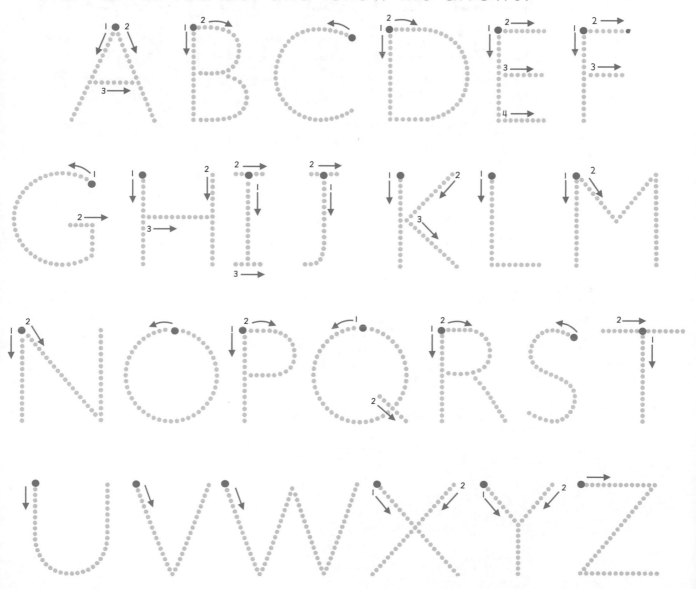

Note for parent: Practice writing your child's name in both lowercase (with a capital to start) and uppercase letters.

61

Writing Capital Letters

Connect the dotted lines for each capital letter and write the matching small one below.

A B C D E F G H I J K L M
a b c d e f g h i j k l m

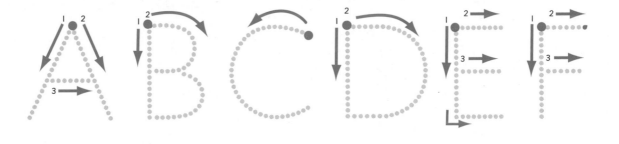

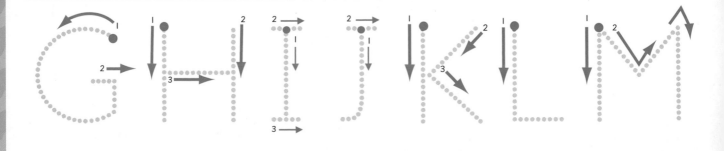

Note for parent: This activity gives your child practice in writing all the capital and lowercase letters. Write the letters in the air with your finger to give further practice.

N O P Q R S T U V W X Y Z

n o p q r s t u v w x y z

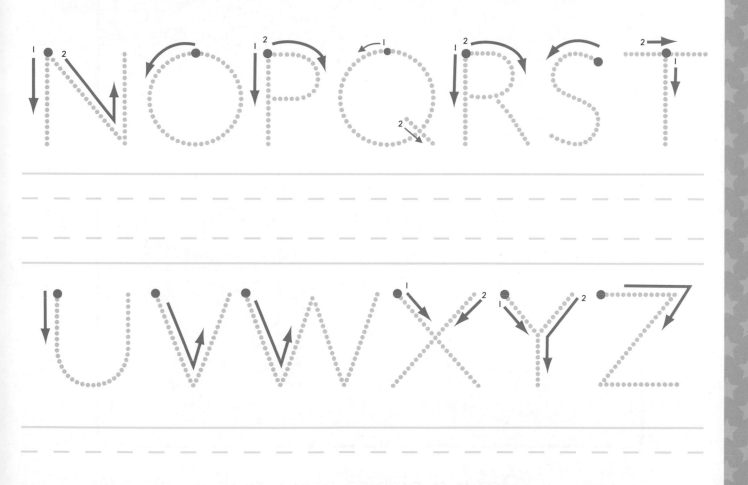

Names

Write your name here, starting with a capital letter.

Draw a picture of yourself.

Choose names for these animals. Write the names below.

Phonics

Helping Your Child

- The activities in this section will help your child learn about phonics. Pictures provide hints and clues to support their understanding.

- Your child will gain the confidence to: blend letters to make words, read words out loud, and begin to spell simple words.

- Your child will learn about: how letters and groups of letters make different sounds, beginning sounds, end sounds, and more.

- Set aside time to do the activities together. Do a little at a time so your child enjoys learning.

- Give lots of encouragement and praise.

- The answers are on pages 310–313.

Contents

Sounding out Letters

Look at the pictures. Say the words. Sound out the beginning letters.

ant	**a**	aaa (not ay)
goat	**g**	guh (not jee)
bat	**b**	b-b-b (not bee)
hat	**h**	hhh (not aitch)
cat	**c**	ck (not see)
igloo	**i**	ih (not eye)
dog	**d**	duh (not dee)
jar	**j**	juh (not jay)
egg	**e**	eh (not ee)
key	**k**	ck (not kay)
fish	**f**	fff (not eff)
log	**l**	lll (not ell)

Note for parent: This activity helps your child to practice phonemes. Encourange your child to focus on the phonetic sound of a letter instead of its name.

| | m | mmm (not em) |
| **mug** | | |

| | t | tuh (not tee) |
| **ten** | | |

| | n | nnn (not en) |
| **nut** | | |

| | u | uh (not you) |
| **umbrella** | | |

| | o | ah (not oh) |
| **octopus** | | |

| | v | vvv (not vee) |
| **van** | | |

| | p | puh (not pee) |
| **pen** | | |

| | w | wuh (not double-you) |
| **web** | | |

| | q | kwuh (not kew) |
| **queen** | | |

| | x | ks (not ex) |
| **bo<u>x</u>** | | |

| | r | rrr (not aar) |
| **ring** | | |

| | y | yuh (not why) |
| **yo-yo** | | |

| | s | sss (not ess) |
| **sun** | | |

| | z | zzz (not zee) |
| **zebra** | | |

Beginning with s

Trace the letter s with a pencil.

I spy with my little eye something beginning with s. Draw a circle around each object that starts with s.

Which object does not start with s?
Draw a cross through the object.

Note for parent: Play I Spy with your child at home to encourage them to look for objects that start with different letter sounds.

Beginning with t

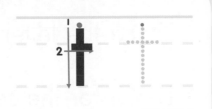

Trace the letter t with a pencil.

Name all the things on the shopping list. What sound do they all start with?

Note for parent: Go for a walk with your child and look for things beginning with the sound t.

71

Trace the letter p with a pencil.

Listen for the sound p at the start of the words:

Peter picked a pot of purple plums.

Name the objects. Draw a circle around each object that starts with p. Draw a cross through each object that does not start with p.

Trace the letter b with a pencil.

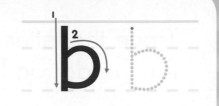

Listen for the sound b at the start
of the words:

Billy eats berries and
beetles for breakfast.

Name the objects. Draw a circle around each
object that starts with b. Draw a cross through
each object that does not start with b.

Note for parent: Encourage your child to say the sound of the letter, not its name—
p is p-p-puh, not pee, and b is b-b-buh, not bee.

73

Letter Sound i

Trace the letter i with a pencil.
Put the dot on last.

Say the sound of each letter, then blend
the sounds together to read each word.

Listen for the sound i in the middle of the words.
Draw a circle around each word that contains i.

Dip, dip, dip,
My little ship,
Big cup and saucer,
Bobbing on the water.
Dip, dip, dip,
My little ship!

Note for parent: Say the short sound of i as in insect, not the long sound as in ice.
Blend is a word that teachers use with children to describe how we connect sounds in words.

Letter Sound n

Trace the letter n with a pencil.

Listen for the sound n at the start and end of the words. Draw a circle around the letter n in each word.

net

pen

nut

bun

ten

sun

Color the pictures.

Note for parent: These activities help your child to listen for sounds at the start, in the middle, and at the end of words.

Say the Sounds: s, a, t, p, i

Trace over the letters. Say the sound of each letter.

s for

a for

p for

t for

i for

Look at the big picture and name something beginning with each of these sounds:

s a t p i

Blend to Make Words

Blend the letter sounds to find out what Rob Robot is saying. Say the words.

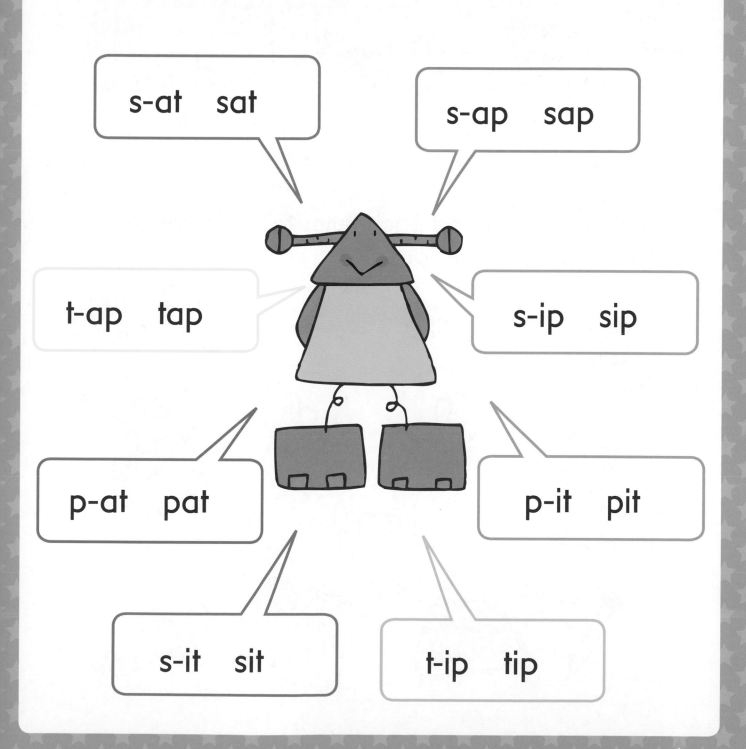

Note for parent: To blend means to join the separate sounds together until the word sounds right.

77

Trace over the letters. Say the sound of each letter as you write it.

n for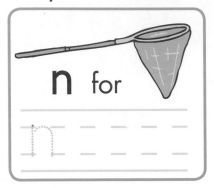

n

m for

m

d for

d

Draw lines to connect each letter to 3 pictures that begin with the same sound.

(n)   (d)   (m)

Blend to Make Words

Blend the letter-sounds to read the words on each mat.
Find 2 words on this page that are **exactly** the same.
Draw a circle around them.

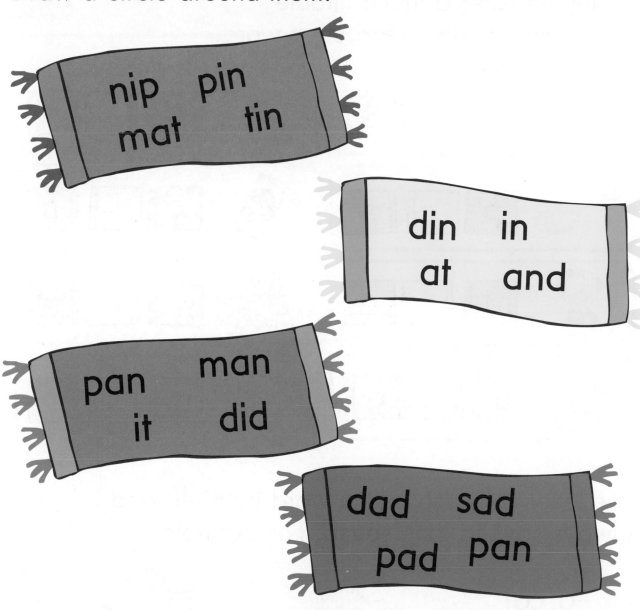

nip pin
mat tin

din   in
at   and

pan   man
it   did

dad   sad
pad   pan

Now find words that end in the same sound.
Draw lines to connect them.

Note for parent: Read aloud the rhyming words with emphasis on the final sounds.
Encourage your child to listen for the rhyme.

Word Building with a

Write the letter a in the middle
of the words. Then read each word.

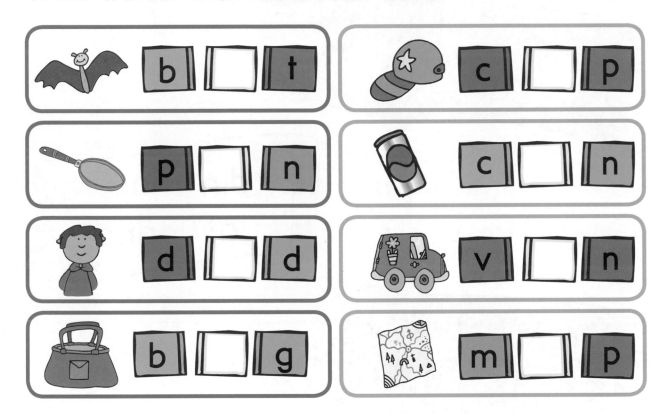

The letter a is also a little word by itself, and it
always says its long sound. For example:

a cat

a rat

Note for parent: Say the short sound of a as in apple, not the long sound as in angel.

Word Building with e and o

Say the sound of each letter, then blend the sounds together to read each word.

Draw a circle around the word that matches each picture.

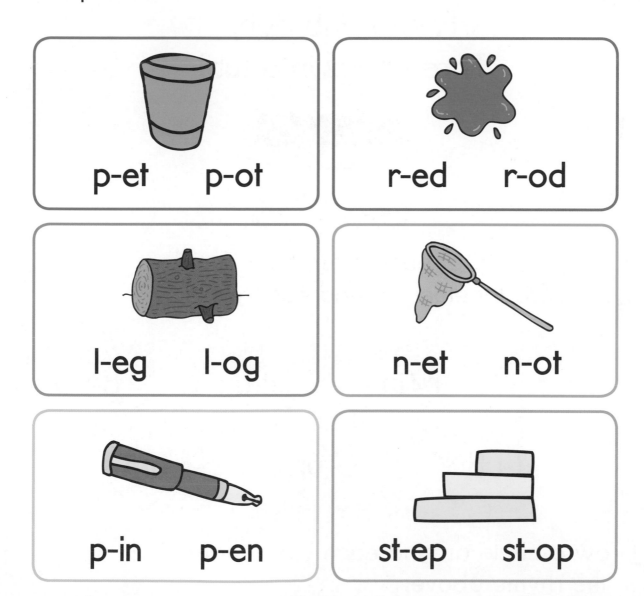

p-et   p-ot

r-ed   r-od

l-eg   l-og

n-et   n-ot

p-in   p-en

st-ep   st-op

Word Building with u

Trace the letter **u** with a pencil.

Listen for the sound **u** in the middle of the words:

Rub-a-dub-dub,
Three pugs in a tub!

Say the sound of each letter, then blend the sounds together to read each word.

h-ut   r-ub   c-up   d-ub

t-ub   b-ut   s-um

Draw a circle around each word that is in the rhyme above.

Note for parent: Say the short sound of u as in under, not the long sound as in unicorn.

Word Building with o and i

Say the sound of each letter, then blend the sounds together to read each word. **ck** makes the sound **k** in all these words.

Draw a line to connect each word to the correct picture.

s-ock

br-ick

l-ock

cl-ock

st-ick

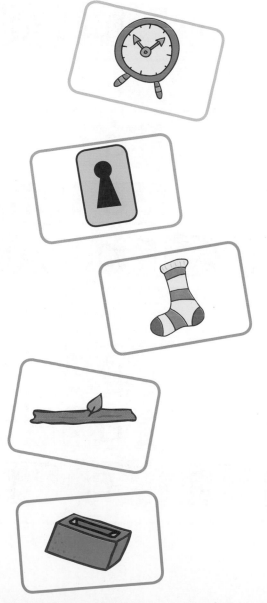

Note for parent: Say the short sound of i as in inventor, not the long sound as in idea. Say the short sound of o as in otter, not the long sound as in oval.

83

Word Builder

Letter sounds are put together to build words.
Read the words in each word wall below.

a

a n

a n d

a

a n

a n t

a

a n

p a n

a

a m

S a m

a

a t

p a t

Note for parent: Look for smaller words within longer words. For example am in Sam.
Can you find any little words in your child's name?

Find 5 words in each word search below. Look across and diagonally. Draw a circle around each word you find in the word search box.

man
sat
tap
tan
map

t	a	p
s	a	t
m	a	n

t	i	p
s	i	t
p	i	n

pin
sit
pip
tin
tip

Note for parent: Word games are a fun way of practicing literacy skills.

85

Vowel Sounds

Look at each picture and say the word. Circle the sound that is in the middle. Write the sound to finish the word.

	a i	p _ n
	e u	b _ s
	o e	l _ g
	a e	w _ b
	e a	c _ t
	i e	n _ t

Note for parent: It can be tricky to hear the sound in the middle. Help your child to read the words by sounding out each letter.

More Vowel Sounds

Say the word in the basket.
Color the balloons with the
same middle sound as the
word in the basket.

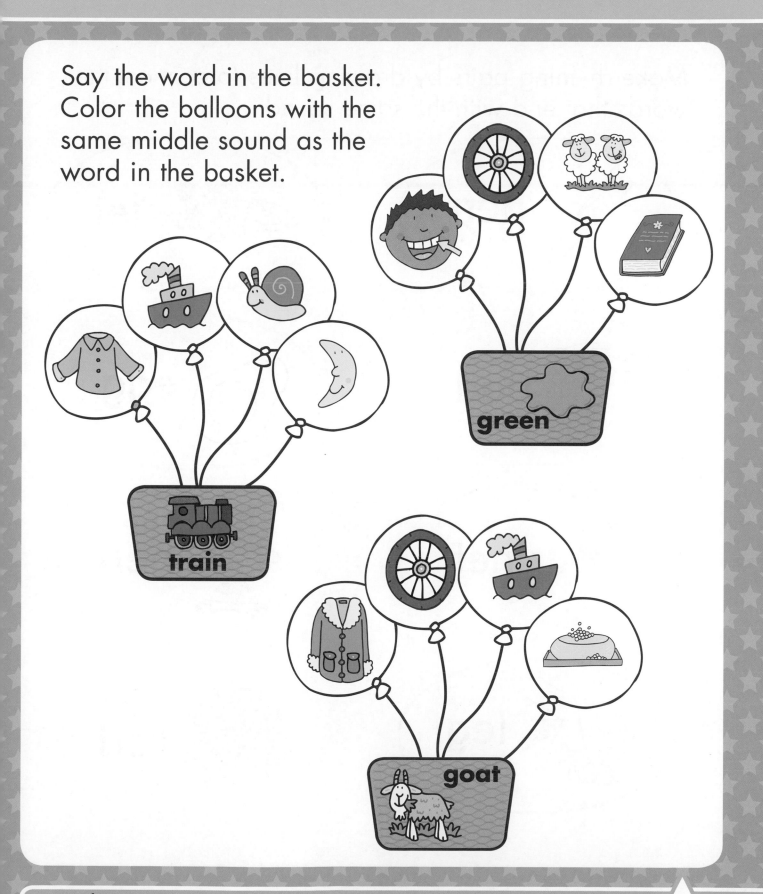

Note for parent: This activity gives your child more practice in recognizing middle sounds and understanding that two letters together can make one sound.

87

Find the Rhymes 1

Make rhyming pairs by drawing lines to connect the words that end with the same sound.

pen

jet

bed

egg

net

hen

leg

red

Note for parent: Read pen in the left-hand column. Then read down the second column until you reach the correct answer hen.

Find the Vowel Sounds

Say the name of each picture. Draw a circle around the letter that comes in the middle of each name.

n __ t

e a

r __ d

a e

h __ n

e h

m __ n

m e

p __ n

t e

w __ b

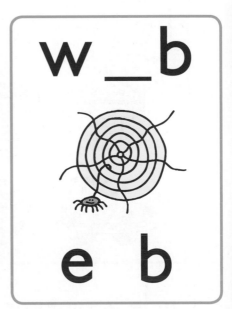

e b

Say the Sounds: g, o, c, k

Trace over the letters. Say the sound of each letter as you write it.

g   g

o   o

c   c

k   k

Circle 2 pictures in each box that begin with the same sound.

Note for parent: The letters c and k sound the same in these words. Point out the different sound of o in orange and owl.

Blend to Make Words

Blend the letter sounds to read the words.

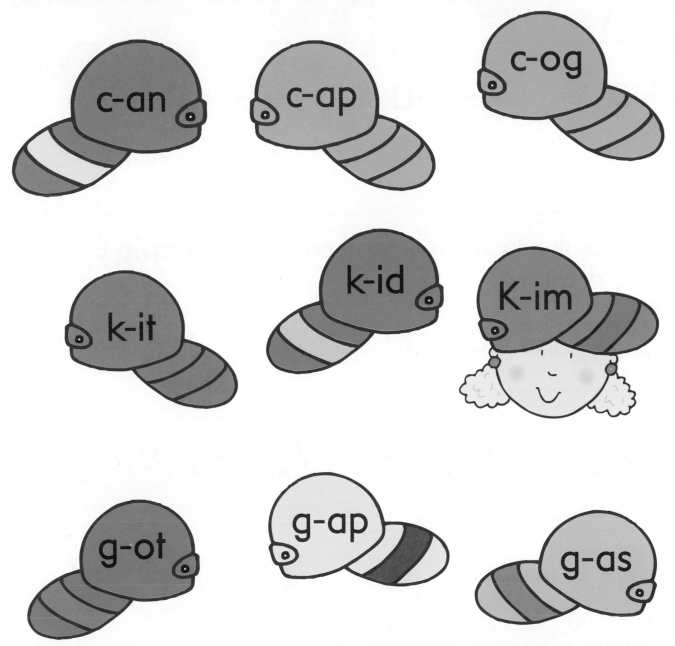

c-an

c-ap

c-og

k-it

k-id

K-im

g-ot

g-ap

g-as

Which of these words has a capital letter? Why?

Note for parent: Tell your child that names begin with capital (or uppercase) letters. Practice writing the capital letter that starts your child's name.

91

Trace over the letters. Say the sound of each letter as you write it.

| e for 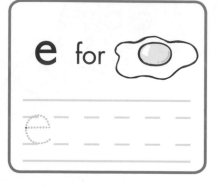 | u for  | r for 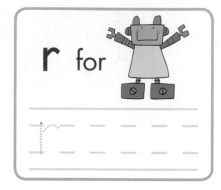 |

e - - - - - -

u - - - - - -

r - - - - - -

Circle the sound you can hear in the **middle** of each word below.

 pen **e** or **u**

 red **e** or **u**

 sun **e** or **u**

 rug **e** or **u**

10 ten **e** or **u**

 cup **e** or **u**

 net **e** or **u**

 nut **e** or **u**

Say the Sound: ck

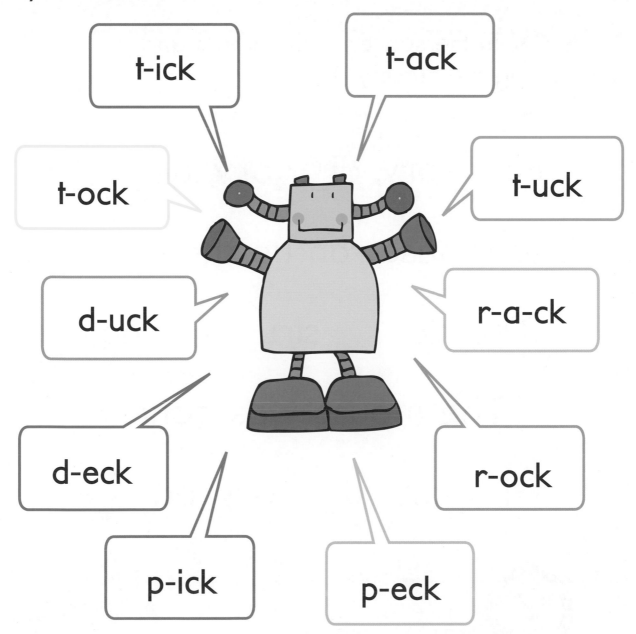

Sometimes we put **c** and **k** together. Blend the letter sounds to find out what Ron Robot is saying. Say the words.

t-ick

t-ack

t-ock

t-uck

d-uck

r-a-ck

d-eck

r-ock

p-ick

p-eck

Draw lines to connect the words that rhyme.

Note for parent: ck is pronounced as one sound. It can also be found in the middle of words, like pocket.

93

Hickory Dickory Dock

Trace over the letters.

ck ck ck ck ck

Write **ck** in the spaces in the words and say or sing the nursery rhyme.

Hi_ _ory, di_ _ory, do_ _,

The mouse ran up the clo_ _,

The clo_ _ stru_ _ one,

The mouse was gone,

Hi_ _ory, di_ _ory, do_ _!

Peter Piper

Say this tongue twister as fast as you can. Get ready!

Peter Piper picked a peck
of pickled peppers!
Where's the peck of pickled peppers
Peter Piper picked?

Find all the **p** sounds in this tongue twister and circle each letter **p**.

Here's another one to try. Say it fast!

She sells seashells
by the sea shore.

Find the Rhymes 2

Draw a line to connect each creature to the food it likes to eat, which starts with the same letter as the creature's name. The first one has been done for you.

 Fred frog likes …  green grass.

 Gretel goat likes …  harvest hay.

 Terrible troll likes …  shiny shrimps.

 Shane shark likes …  fresh flies.

 Harry horse likes …  tasty toads.

Note for parent: Words in a sentence starting with the same letter are called alliterations, like a tall tree. Look out for examples.

Find the Rhymes 3

Make rhyming pairs by drawing lines to connect the words that end with the same sound.

 sock

 chick

 black

 peck

 brick

 sack

 truck

 clock

 neck

 duck

Note for parent: All these words end in ck. Ask your child to listen for the middle sounds to find the rhyme. It's a bit more difficult.

97

Say the Sounds: l, h, b, f

Trace over the letters. Say the sound of each letter as you write it.

l for

h for

b for

f for

Sound out the letters in these words. Read the words.

leg

log

hut

hat

bed

bat

fin

fan

Note for parent: Sound out the letters in each word. Then blend to say the word.

Match Letters to Pictures

Say the sound of the letter in the middle of each circle. Draw lines to connect each letter to 3 pictures in the big circle that begin with this letter.

Note for parent: Prompt your child to find the answer. Help them by pointing to each letter and saying their sounds.

99

Double ff

What is the wolf saying?

Listen for the sound **ff** at the end of the words:

Ruff!

Try to read the words yourself.

sn-iff

c-uff

p-uff

st-uff

cl-iff

fl-uff

Note for parent: Read these words aloud with your child, then close the book. How many words can your child remember?

Double ss

What is the snake saying?

Try to read the words yourself.

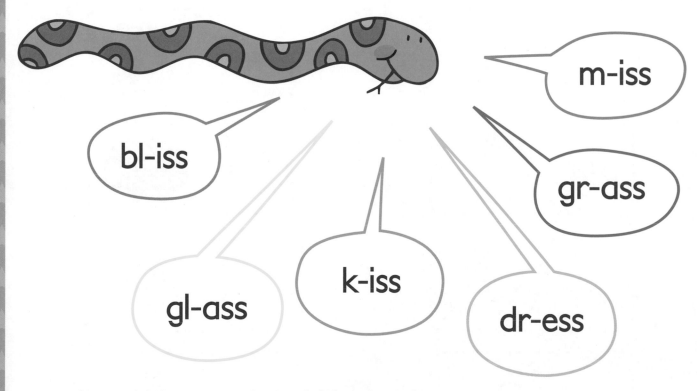

Color each speech bubble that has
a word that ends with **iss**.

Note for parent: Ask your child: Can you make up a sentence with any of these words in it?

101

Beginning Sounds

Say the name of each picture. Connect the things that begin with the same sound.

snake		s		table
apple		a		jam
ten		t		panda
jar		j		nest
pig		p		sun
net		n		ant

Note for parent: This activity gives your child practice in listening for beginning sounds. Encourage your child to say the sound of the letter, not its name—s is sss, not ess.

cat

elephant

hat

fish

rat

moon

dog

c

e

h

f

r

m

d

fox

monkey

duck

cup

egg

rabbit

hand

Words That Rhyme

Say the name of the picture on each card.
Match the white cards with words that rhyme
on colored cards and then color them the same.

mouse

car

bat

key

boat

frog

house

star

cat

tree

coat

dog

Note for parent: This activity helps your child to hear end sounds that rhyme. Ask your child to say each word out loud. Can they think of other words that rhyme?

Match the Rhymes

Say the name of the animal on each envelope.
Circle the picture that rhymes with it.

To
Mr. Fox

To
Miss Bee

3

To
Mrs. Bear

To
Mr. Rat

Note for parent: Encourage your child to explore more rhyming words. Make up silly sentences about each animal. For example: Mr. Rat sat on a fat cat.

Make New Words

Make new words by changing the beginning sounds. Use the letters in the box and the pictures to help you.

h f r c s m

 map

 _ap

 bun

 _un

pen

 _en

 hat

 _at

 rug

 _ug

 van

 _an

Note for parent: This activity shows your child that rhyming words can be made by changing the beginning sound.

Find the Sounds

Connect each letter to the things in the picture that begin with the same sound.

f   s   c   b

Make up a story about what is happening in the picture.

Blend the sounds together to make words. Draw lines to connect the sounds to the complete words. The first one has been done for you.

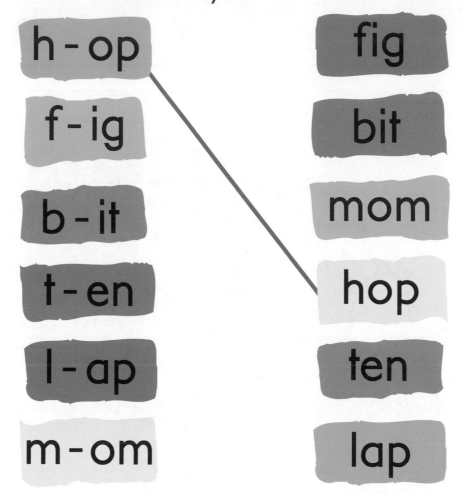

h - op
f - ig
b - it
t - en
l - ap
m - om

fig
bit
mom
hop
ten
lap

Make some nonsense words by joining these sounds. Say the words.

b - im   t - as   l - ib

s - ut   f - ep   h - of

Note for parent: The nonsense words are a good test of your child's phonic skills.

Complete the Words

Blend the sounds together. Trace the letters to complete the words.

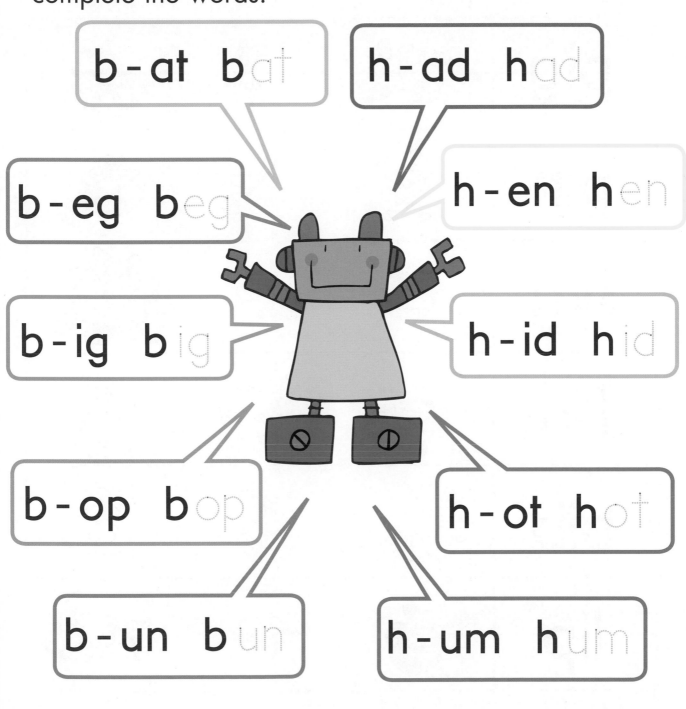

b-at bat

h-ad had

b-eg beg

h-en hen

b-ig big

h-id hid

b-op bop

h-ot hot

b-un bun

h-um hum

Circle the Picture 1

Circle the picture that matches the word on the left.

pig			
pin			
big			
fin			
bib			
lip			

Note for parent: Sound out the letters in each word then say the word. Look along the row for a matching picture.

Connect the Sounds 1

Say the sound of the letters in the middle of each box. Draw lines to connect the sound to the pictures in the box that end with this sound.

Note for parent: Read the letters in the middle of each box as one sound. Say the names of the pictures in a clockwise direction.

111

Read the List

Read the items on the list. Tick each one as you find it in Sid's suitcase. Is anything missing?

ball ☐

bell ☐

doll ☐

cup ☐

pin ☐

pen ☐

cap ☐

bat ☐

fan ☐

Circle the item that is on the list but not in his suitcase!

Note for parent: This activity will revise phonemes already introduced.

Circle the Words

Circle the correct word to match each picture.

ten or **den**

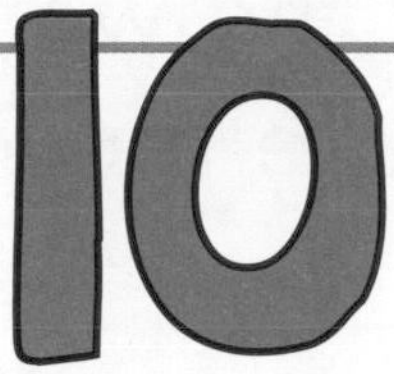

10

dog or **cog**

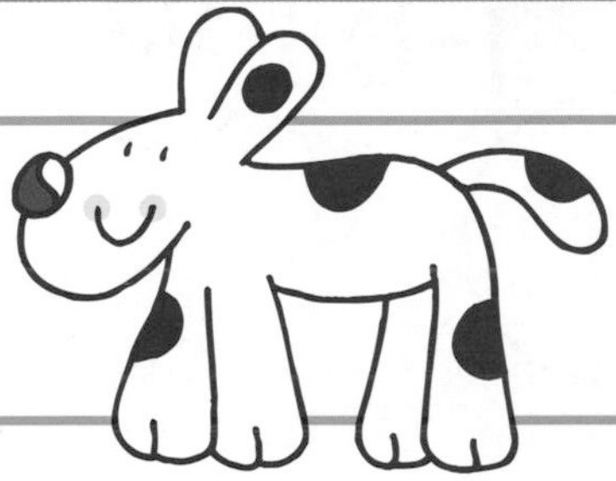

sup or **up**

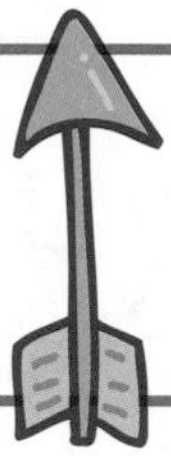

fan or **can**

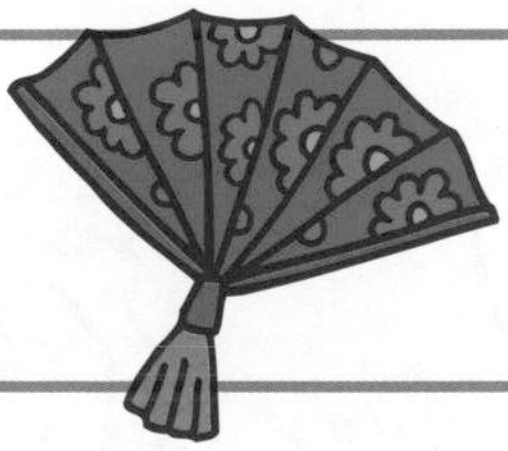

mop or **top**

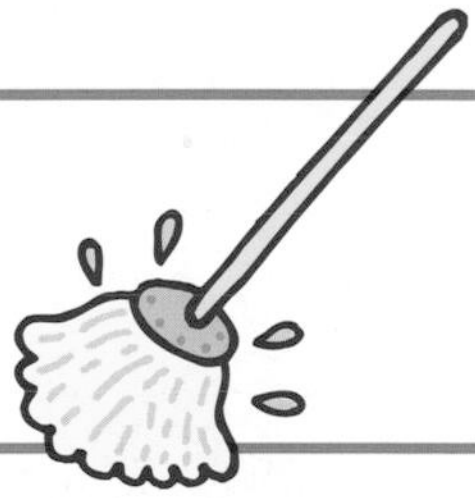

sock or **lock**

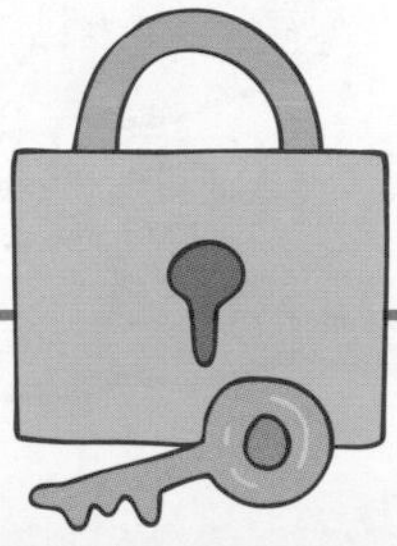

Color the Real Words

Say each letter sound, then blend the sounds together to read the word. Which words are nonsense and which are real? Color the real words in red.

i-b (ib) a-t (at)

i-f (if)

o-n (on)

u-g (ug)

a-m (am)

u-p (up)

i-n (in)

Note for parent: This activity provides further practice in blending sounds and decoding unfamiliar words.

Name the Robots

Say each letter sound, then blend the sounds together to read the words.

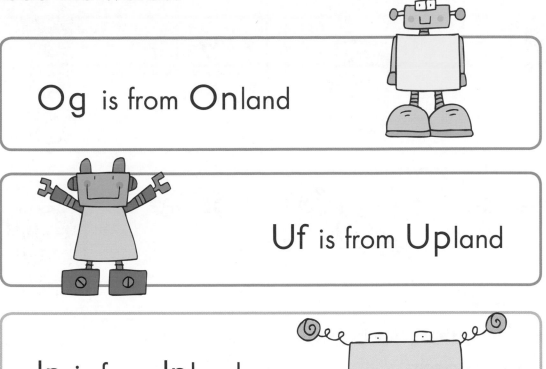

Og is from Onland

Uf is from Upland

Ip is from Inland

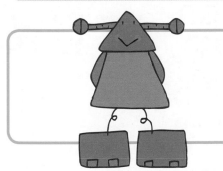

Um is from Ugland

Who is from Inland?   Who is from Onland?

Say the Sounds: j, v, w, x

Trace over the letters. Say the sound of each letter as you write it.

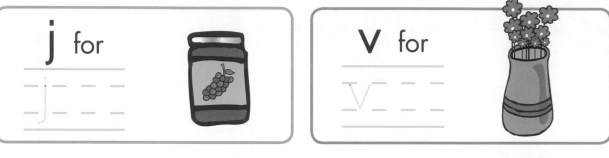

j for

v for

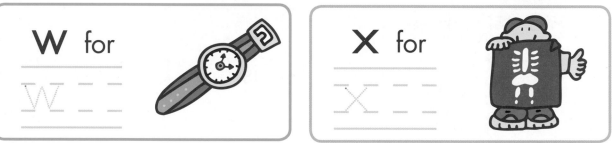

w for

x for

Trace the letters to complete the words.
Read the words.

jar

jug

van

vet

web

witch

box

fox

Note for parent: Few words in the English language begin with x. It is more common as a final sound.

Pet Names

Match the pets to their owners. Their names start with the same letters. Draw lines to connect them.

Jack and ...   Bix

Raj and ...   Van

Tim and ...   Jaws

Pip and ...   Mug

Vin and ...   Pop

Bex and ...   Rav

Meg and ...   Tom

Note for parent: Alliteration (a string of words with the same beginning consonant sounds, like Jack and Jaws) is a common literary device.

Say the Words

Say each word and look at what the children are doing. Can you find an example of each word in the big picture?

jog hop pop mop box

Note for parent: Ask your child to listen for the sound that is in all these words. What is it? (The o sound.)

Circle the First Letter

Look at each picture and draw a circle around the letter that comes at the beginning of each word. Try to write the letters in the correct spaces to finish the words.

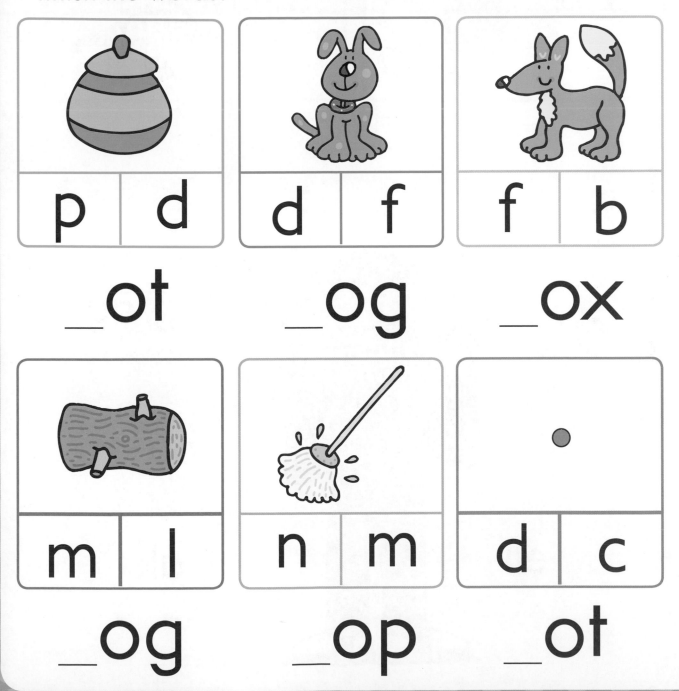

p | d

_ot

d | f

_og

f | b

_ox

m | l

_og

n | m

_op

d | c

_ot

Note for parent: Teach your child to write the letters of the alphabet and practice the letters in his/her name.

Say the Sounds: y, z, zz

Trace over the letters. Say the sound of each letter as you write it.

yes

zip

fizz

zigzag

zero

buzz

yell

yak

Note for parent: Many times when z comes at the end of a word, it's doubled.

Trace over the letters. These two letters make one sound when they are together.

qu   qu   qu   qu

Write **qu** in the spaces in the words and say the rhyme.

Qu is for _ _iver and _ _ake,

But not for shiver and shake,

Qu is for _ _arrel and _ _ibble

But not for dribble and drabble

Qu is for _ _ick and _ _ack,

Queen and _ _iet,

Quarry and _ _ite,

Quiz and _ _est,

Are there any more "q"s?

Join the _ _eue!

Note for parent: The letters q and u are usually found together in the English language.

121

Connect the Sounds 2

Say the sound of the letters in the middle of each box. Draw lines to connect the sound to the pictures in the box that end with the same sound.

Note for parent: Read the letters in the middle of each box as one sound. Say the names of the pictures in a clockwise direction.

Match the Names

Draw lines to connect the books to the children.

Pat   Jaz   Dan   Ann

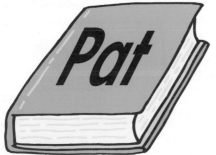 

Find the Rhymes 4

Make rhyming pairs by drawing lines to connect the words that end with the same sound.

 rug

 drum

 bull

 bun

 sun

 mug

 nut

 pull

 plum

 cut

Find the sh Sounds

Say each word. What sound can you hear at the beginning of all these words? Look at the big picture and find an example of each word.

ship	shells	shore
shop	shark	shoe

Note for parent: Pronounce sh as a single sound, not as two separate sounds s and h. This is known as a blend.

125

Circle the Picture 2

Circle the picture that matches the word on the left.

dish			
fish			
bush			
push			
sash			
cash			

Note for parent: Remember to pronounce s and h together as one sound sh. For example, dish has three sounds—d-i-sh.

Connect the Sounds 3

Say the sound of the letters in the middle of each box. Draw lines to connect the sound to the pictures in the box that contain this sound.

Circle ng or nk

Say the name of each picture. Circle the sound you can hear at the end of each word.

ng   nk

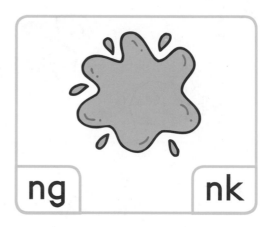

ng   nk

ng   nk

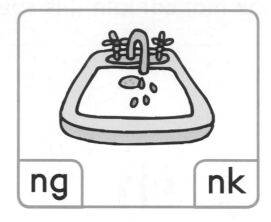

ng   nk

ng   nk

ng   nk

Note for parent: ng and nk are common word endings so it is important to learn to distinguish between them.

Say the name of each picture. Write the missing letter to finish each word. Choose from these letters:

d g l m n s t x

su_

dol_

fro_

mo_

ba_

si_

be_

bu_

Note for parent: You could ask your child to write the letter that ends their name in the space on this page.

Catch the Ball

Draw lines to connect the words that are the same.

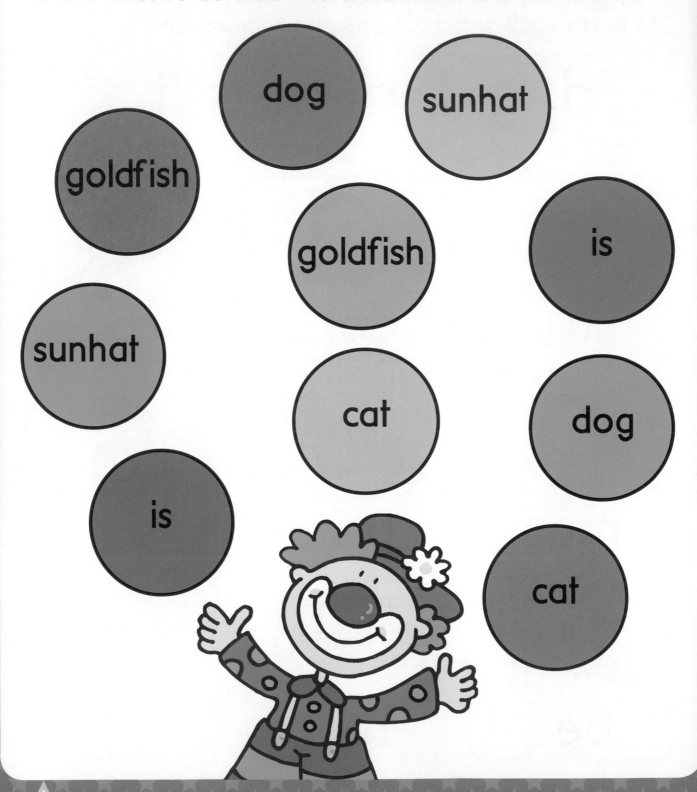

Note for parent: Point to the words and read them aloud. Draw attention to the different lengths of the words.

Circle the Picture 3

Circle the picture that matches the word on the left.

mat			
can			
dad			
pan			
van			
bat			

Note for parent: Sound out the letters in each word, then say the word. Look along the row for a matching picture.

131

Circle the Picture 4

Circle the picture that matches the word on the left.

pen			
bed			
pig			
red			
ten			
web			

Note for parent: Use the adjective red combined with other words that go with it to make a phrase, like a red bus.

Fishing Fun

Look carefully at the letters in the words. Connect the words that are exactly the same.

Note for parent: These words look similar at first glance. Encourage your child to focus on the initial letters.

133

Draw the Lines

Draw a line to connect each word to the correct picture.

can

fin

lid

pig

pin

bib

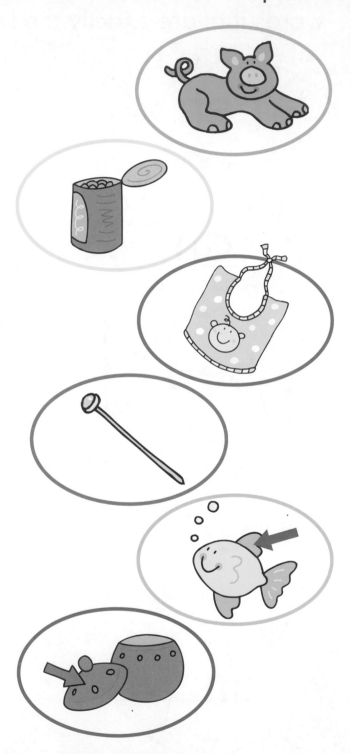

Note for parent: Help to sound out the letters in each word. Don't worry if your child confuses p and g at first.

Circle the Word

Look at each picture then draw a circle around the correct word.

kid | **kit**

pip | **bib**

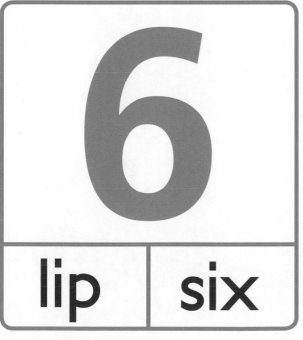

lip | **six**

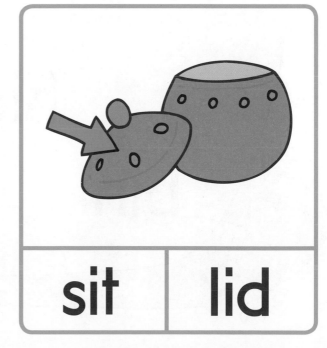

sit | **lid**

Snail Rhymes

Draw lines to connect pairs of words that rhyme.

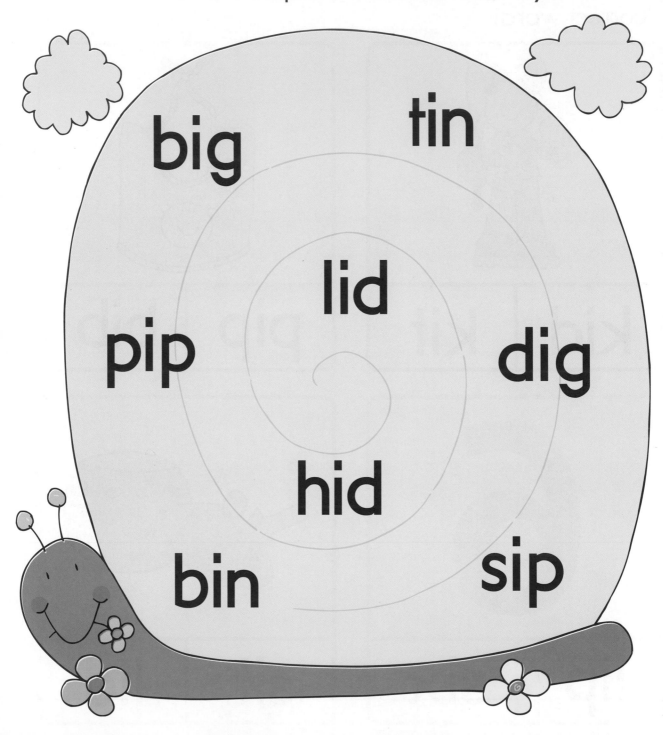

Say the Names

Say the animals' names. Who is going to win the race? Who will be last?

Note for parent: You might want to talk about uppercase letters (capitals) and lowercase letters. Say that names begin with uppercase letters.

137

Reading and Language Arts

Helping Your Child

- The activities in this section will help your child to learn about reading and language. Pictures provide hints and clues to support their understanding.

- Your child will gain the confidence to read common high-frequency words by sight and analyze and decode words.

- Your child will learn about: capitals, upper and lower case letters, nouns, and verbs.

- Set aside time to do the activities together. Do a little at a time so that your child enjoys learning.

- Give lots of encouragement and praise.

- The answers are on pages 313—315.

Contents

Draw the Words

Read the descriptions.
Draw the animals.

One day we went for a walk
and we saw …

… a big, buzzing,
busy bee

… a spotty, slippery,
slithering snake

… a pair of pretty,
pink pigs

… and four funny,
floppy fish.

Note for parent: This activity practices beginning sounds and comprehension. Have fun describing other animals your child might have seen.

Find the Words

Find the words in the puzzle. Color them in.

b	x	e	s	j	k
e	y	t	p	a	n
d	a	v	n	a	b
z	m	o	m	q	h
c	f	n	l	u	i
a	o	g	p	a	j
t	r	n	e	t	a
d	a	d	w	d	r

~~mom~~

dad

bed

pan

jar

cat

net

Write the words.

Note for parent: This activity gives your child practice in CVC words – consonant, vowel, consonant. Some words go across and some go down.

Sounds at the End

Say the name of each picture. Color the letter that makes the sound at the end of the word.

p b   m n   p d

g k   t c   b d

x n   m k   n m

Note for parent: This activity helps your child to listen for the final sound in a word. Encourage your child to think of other words that end in the same sounds.

More Than One

Add an **S** sound at the end of a word when there is more than one thing.

 hat

 hats

Write the missing words.

1 car

2 _ _ _ _

1 bee

4 _ _ _ _

1 egg

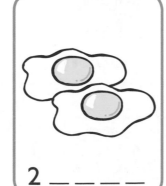

2 _ _ _ _ _

1 rug

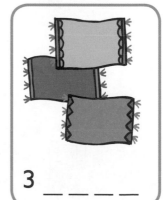

3 _ _ _ _ _

Note for parent: This activity helps your child understand plurals (more than one), starting with simple plurals, where you just add s.

Opposites

Read the words in each row. Circle the word that has the opposite meaning to the first word.

big **sad** **small** **wet**

empty **full** **thin** **dirty**

old **high** **open** **new**

on **night** **up** **off**

Note for parent: Learning opposites helps your child to understand their meanings. Ask your child guess the opposites to all the words on the page.

What Happens Next

Draw what you think happens next.

Note for parent: This activity helps your child to develop the idea of telling a simple story with a beginning, middle, and ending.

145

Catch the Ball

Look at the balls. Find pairs of words that are the same. Draw lines to connect the words.

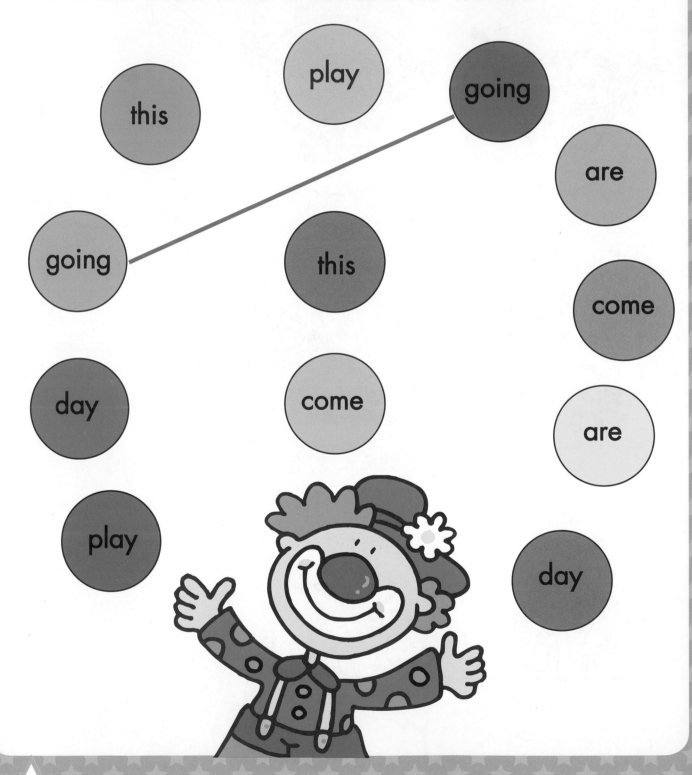

Note for parent: Praise your child's efforts as they read these high-frequency words.

Three-Letter Words

Read the words. Draw a circle around the word that matches each picture.

cat
cot

pin
pen

fun
fan

dog
dig

man
mom

day
dad

peg
pig

cup
cap

Snakes and Ladders

Draw lines to connect the same words on each ladder.

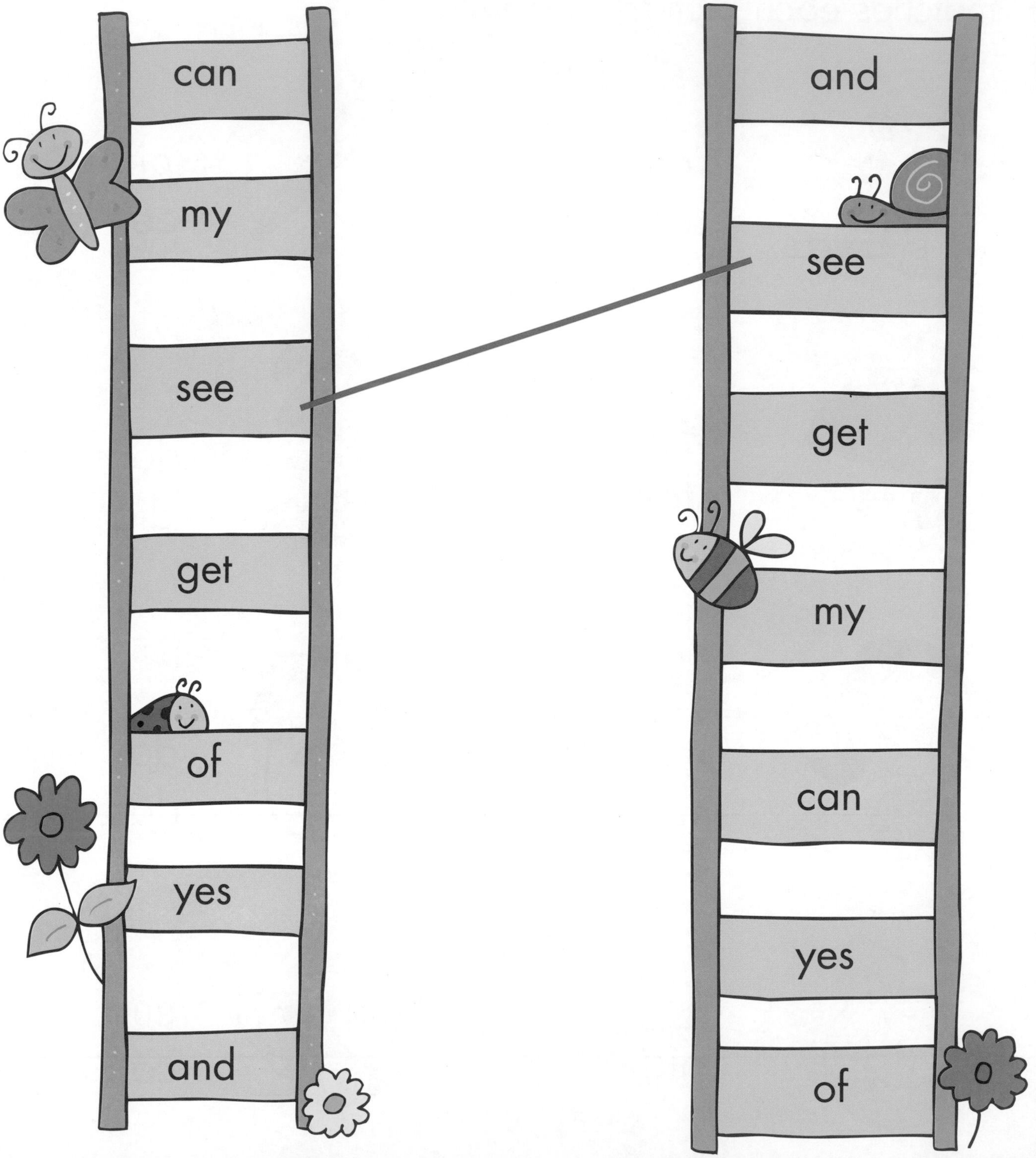
can
my
see
get
of
yes
and
and
see
get
my
can
yes
of

Note for parent: This activity gives more practice in reading high-frequency words.

Draw lines to connect the same words on each snake.

Color the Words

Find pairs of words that are the same.
Color each pair a different color.

and	back	said	she
the	went	look	they
look	they	and	went
said	she	the	back

How many of the words above can you find
in these sentences?
Draw a circle around each one.

A boy and a girl went to the pet shop.

The girl said she liked the puppy.

They went back to look at the puppy.

Note for parent: This activity gives your child practice with common high-frequency words.
Explain that the word at the start of a sentence begins with a capital letter.

Find the little words in the big words.
Circle the little words.

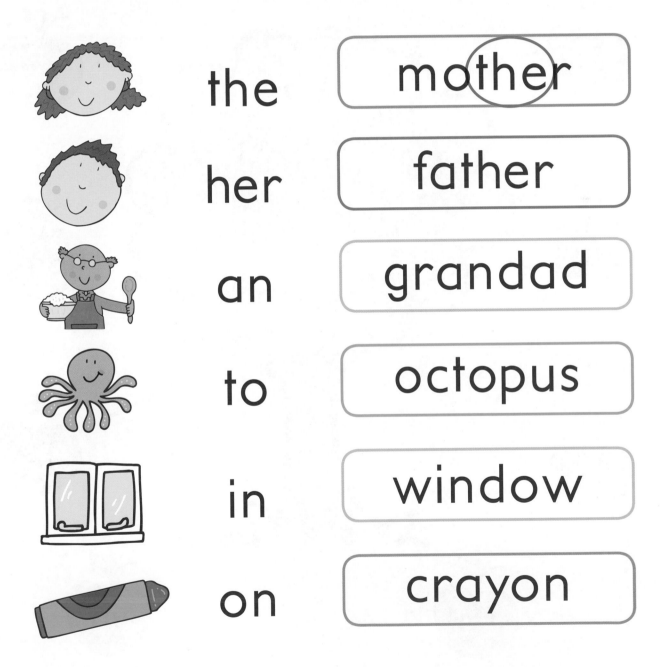

the   mother

her   father

an   grandad

to   octopus

in   window

on   crayon

Note for parent: Looking for little words in bigger words helps your child with word recognition and spelling. Find other little words in these words.

151

Real Words

Read the words in the tree. Connect each word to the right apple.

Note for parent: This activity gives more practice in high-frequency words.

Read the words in the rocket. Connect each word to the right star.

House Words

Look at the picture. Write in the missing words.

 This is a _ _ _ _ _ .

 This is a _ _ _ _ .

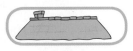 This is a _ _ _ _ _ _ .

 This is a _ _ _ _ .

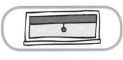 This is a _ _ _ _ _ _ .

Note for parent: You can also help your child write your house number on the door in the picture.

Missing Words

Use the words in the boxes to complete the sentences.
Write them in place.

> is   a   cat

This is my ....

It .... white.

It has ....long tail.

> can   dog   big

This is a ....

It .... bark.

It is ....

Sentences

Use the pictures and words to complete the sentences.

coat   door   desk   chair   dinosaur   bed   net

The coat is on the back of the d _ _ _.

The n _ _ is under the bed.

The d _ _ _ _ _ _ _ is on the bed.

The chair is near the d _ _ _.

Capital Letters

Look at these names. They all begin with a capital letter.

| Jack | Emma | Oliver | Lily |

Draw lines to connect the capital letters to the small letters.

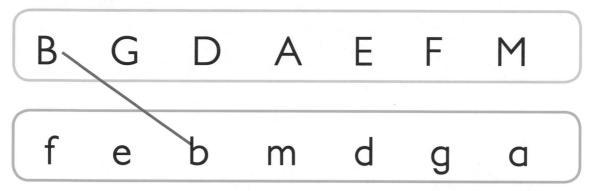

B   G   D   A   E   F   M

f   e   b   m   d   g   a

Circle all the capital letters in the puzzle.

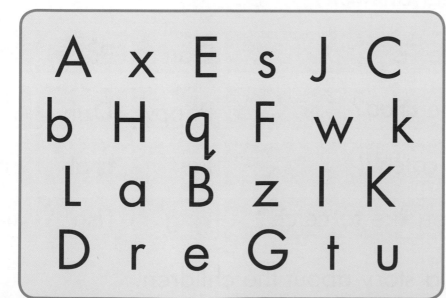

A x E s J C
b H q F w k
L a B z l K
D r e G t u

Note for parent: Tell your child that names always begin with a capital letter. Together, write out the names of people in your family.

157

Tell the Story

Trace the fishing lines to see what each person has caught.

Dan **Mia** **Ali** **Poppy**

Circle the correct answer.

Who caught the fish?	Dan	Poppy	Mia
Who caught the crab?	Poppy	Dan	Ali
What did Dan catch?	key	crab	ring
What would you like to catch?	ring	fish	crab

Now make up a story about the children.

Note for parent: This activity encourages your child to look carefully. Read the questions to your child.

Odd One Out

Say the words in each group. Listen to the sounds.
Circle the odd one out in each group.

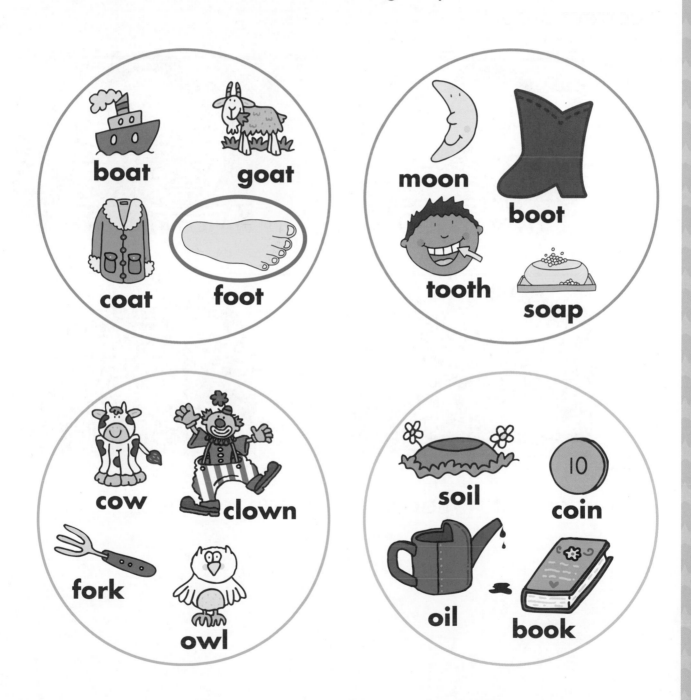

boat   goat

coat   foot

moon   boot

tooth   soap

cow   clown

fork   owl

soil   coin

oil   book

Note for parent: Say the words with your child and listen carefully to the different sounds.
The sounds that are the same may come at the beginning, middle, or end of the word.

Make a Story

Look at the four pictures to see what is happening.
Write the numbers 1 to 4 in the boxes to show their
correct order.

Draw or write what you think happens next.

Note for parent: This activity gives your child practice in story sequencing. Talk about what is happening in each picture. Work out the order of the story.

Word Shapes

Look at the shapes of these words. Write the words in the matching boxes.

little they what some like
when said have was all do

Note for parent: This activity gives your child practice in learning some tricky high-frequency words. The shape of a word can help your child recognize it when reading.

161

Word Puzzle

Count the letters in the words. Draw lines to connect each word to the right train car.

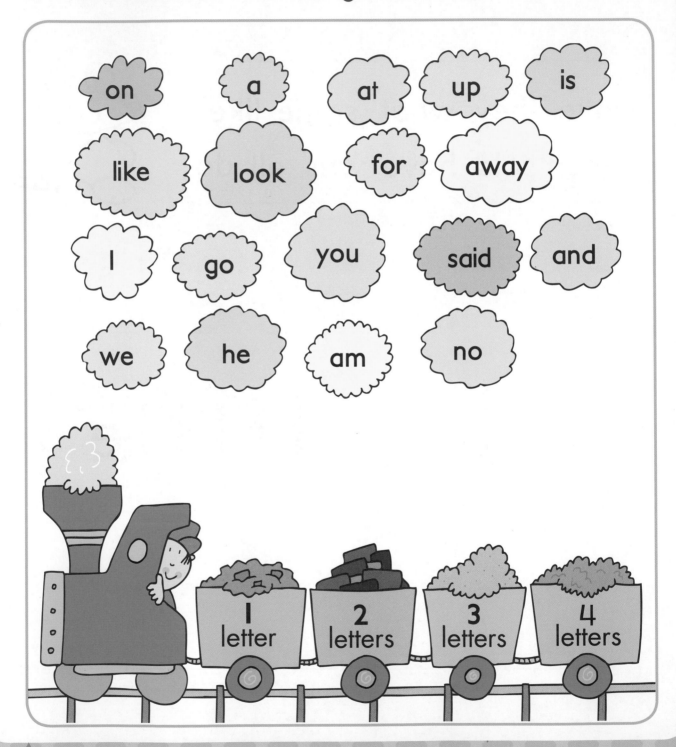

on a at up is

like look for away

I go you said and

we he am no

1 letter   2 letters   3 letters   4 letters

Note for parent: This activity gives your child practice with common high-frequency words.

I Can Read

Can you read and write all the words on this snail?

all
....

dog
....

big
....

of
....

it
....

yes
....

she
....

was
....

me
....

in
....

get
....

can
....

see
....

my
....

went
....

Note for parent: More practice in reading and writing common sight words.

163

Complete the Story

Look at the picture and write the missing words.

The mouse pulls the ....

The cat pulls the ....

The .... pulls the turnip.

They pull and pull and pull and yes!

Here it comes!

Connect the Words

Say the word in each balloon. Draw a line to connect the ones that are the same.

my

an

I

is

it

and

it

I

my

is

an

a

and

a

Note for parent: Learning little words can be just as difficult as learning longer ones.

165

Sight Words I

Some words are not easy to blend. You need to learn these words by memory. See if you can remember these useful words:

the was I my no to go

Read the story below. Trace over the words with a pencil to complete the story.

It was a cold morning.

I put on my hat.

I went to the store for milk.

But the store had no milk.

I had to go home.

Read the sentences below. Choose the correct word to complete each sentence.
Write the words on the lines.

(am)　(at)　(on)

I .... five.

I .... good .... reading.

I can read the words .... this page.

Now try to read the sentences yourself. Trace over the words with a pencil to complete the sentences.

I am five.

I am good at reading.

I can read the words on this page.

Read the Labels

Read the labels.

 a hen in
a pen

 a dog
in the fog

 a cat
on a mat

Answer these questions about the labels.
Draw a ring around each correct answer.

Where is the dog?

on a mat	in the fog	in a pen

Where is the hen?

in the fog	on a mat	in a pen

Where is the cat?

in a pen	on a mat	in the fog

Note for parent: This activity will help your child's comprehension skills—supporting their understanding of what they read with use of memorable rhyme.

Read the Directions

Read the directions.

 Get off the bus.

Go down the path.

Go up to the top of the hill.

 Go in the cave.

Get the gold!

  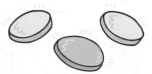

Now see how many directions you can remember from memory.

Rhyming Words

Words that rhyme have the same ending sounds.

Listen for the sound **at** at the end of the words:

Rat-a-tat-tat! Who is that?

A cat in a hat!

Read the words on the hats. Draw a circle around each word that ends with **at**.

cat   mat   but   bat   rat

pot   pat   man   hat

Note for parent: Look for books with predictable rhymes to read with your child. Stop reading when you come to the rhyming word and ask your child to guess which word it will be.

Read the words on the stepping stones. Draw a circle around each word that ends with **ail**.

Now color all the rhyming **ail** stones to make a path across the water.

Note for parent: Say a simple word such as dog, rug, or red and see how many words your child can say that rhyme with it!

Read the Poem

Read the poem. Look at the picture and choose the correct word to complete each sentence. Write the words on the lines.

moon   dog   cakes   sun

My best friend lives on the ....
I hope to visit him quite soon.

We'll go for moon walks with his .... ,
And float in spacesuits in moon fog.

We'll make chocolate moon bars and crater .... ,
And eat rocket lollies and lunar flakes.

But best of all for having fun,
We'll play hide-and-seek with the ....

Now read the poem again.

Note for parent: Stop when you come to the missing word and ask your child to guess the word.

Answer these questions about the poem.
Draw a circle around each correct answer.

Where does the best friend live?

| in the sea | on a farm | on the moon |

Who will they go for moon walks with?

| his dog | his cat | his rabbit |

Who will they play hide-and-seek with?

| the moon | the stars | the sun |

Sound Story: ss, ll, ff

Trace over the letters to complete the words.
Say the sounds as you write them.

ss ll ff

Ask an adult to read the story to you.

Miss Hill rings the bell.

The class play pass the ball.

Bill falls in the grass.

He hears a hiss!

Then a huff and puff!

"Don't fuss," says Miss Hill.

"But, Miss!" says Bill.

"It's behind you!"

"Run, class!" shouts

Miss Hill.

Note for parent: As you read aloud, point to the words with your finger. Then go back to the text and encourage your child to read the double-letter words.

Sight Words 2

Blend the letter sounds to read the story.
Say these sight words:

I   go   no   to   the   of

The bus can go to the top
of the hill.

I can go to the top.

I can hop on the top.

The dog can run on the top.

Oh no, the bus hit a rock on the
top of the hill.

Oh no, the bus cannot go!

Note for parent: The sight words appear at the top of the page. Repetition of these words in the story will help your child to remember them.

175

Compound Words

Connect two words to make one word.
Trace over the letters.

sun - set	sunset
sun - tan	suntan
hand - bag	handbag
hill - top	hilltop
up - on	upon
bath - tub	bathtub
pad - lock	padlock
back - pack	backpack

Note for parent: These words are known as compound words. There are further examples later in the book.

The Grand Old Duke of York

Say the nursery rhyme.

The Grand Old Duke of York,
He had ten thousand men,
He marched them up
To the top of the hill
And he marched them down again....
When they were up they were up,
When they were down they were down.
And when they were only halfway up,
They were neither up nor down!

Where did the Grand Old Duke of York take his men?
Read the signs. Color in the correct sign.

To the top of the rock   >

To the big red bus   >

To the top of the hill   >

Note for parent: Teach your child some well-known nursery rhymes. The language patterns found within them are a good literacy tool.

Read It Yourself

Read the words underneath each picture.

a pig in the mud

a dog in the sun

a cat in a hat

a rat on the run!

Draw your own picture in the last box to match the last description.

Note for parent: Encourage your child to write captions for their drawings.

Find the Word

Look at the pictures and find the correct word to complete each label. Draw lines to connect the words.

cats and

pans

bats and

mugs

pots and

eggs

cups and

dogs

hens and

balls

Note for parent: Discuss these common pairings with your child.

179

Sight Words 3

Say these sight words. They are not easy to sound out so you just have to learn them by sight. They are important because we use them a lot!

Note for parent: There is no easy way of learning these words. But with practice and familiarity your child will begin to recognize them on sight.

Read the speech balloons to find out what they are saying.

They all did it.

It was you.

It was her.

Yes, it was me.

Note for parent: What do you think the children are talking about? Encourage your child to think of possible scenarios.

Read the Poem

Write the letters **ight** in the spaces to complete the words in the poem.

Fright night!

Late last n _ _ _ _ ,

I had a fr _ _ _ _,

I turned on the l _ _ _ _,

The sky was br_ _ _ _,

I pulled the covers t _ _ _ _,

And hid from s _ _ _ _,

Thunder and l _ _ _ _ ning

Is so fr _ _ _ _ ening!

Then out came the morning sun

With golden boxing gloves on,

The sun won the f _ _ _ _,

Everything was alr _ _ _ _.

Note for parent: It is easy to write your own poems in this way by using one rhyming sound and repeating it on every line.

Answer the Questions

Read the questions. Circle **yes** or **no**.

Can a duck read?   yes   no

Can a dog cry?   yes   no

Can a cat play bingo?   yes   no

Can apples be blue?   yes   no

Can you ride a bike?   yes   no

Can you say a rhyme?   yes   no

Can ice melt?   yes   no

Can the sun freeze?   yes   no

Note for parent: Together you can make up some more questions and try them out on family and friends.

183

Counting

Helping Your Child

- The activities in this section will help your child learn about counting. Pictures provide hints and clues to support their understanding.

- Your child will gain the confidence to: count up to 10 and 20 fluently.

- Your child will learn about: counting, comparing, and how to form numbers correctly.

- Set aside time to do the activities together. Do a little at a time so that your child enjoys learning.

- Give lots of encouragement and praise.

- The answers are on pages 315—316.

Contents

Match the Socks

Count the spots on each sock. Draw lines to connect the socks with the same number of spots.

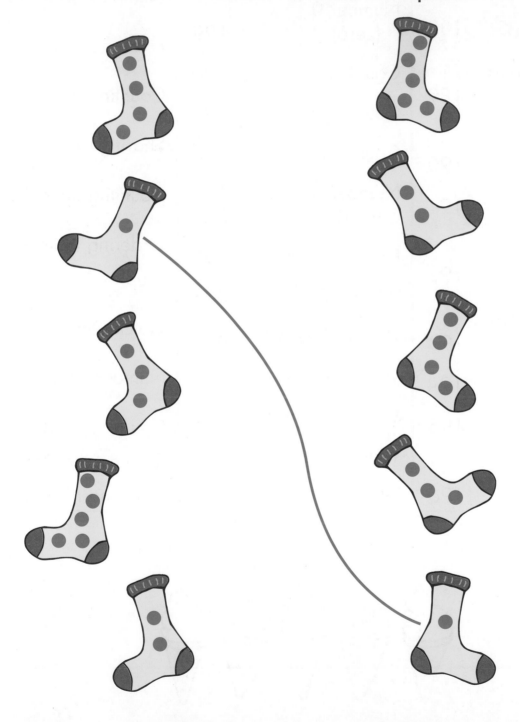

Note for parent: Identifying numbers that are the same or different prepares your child for adding and subtracting.

What's Missing?

Write the missing numbers.

Draw the missing things.

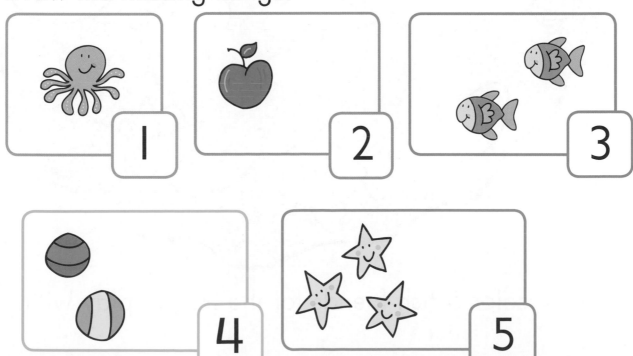

Note for parent: Working out the missing objects prepares your child for adding and subtracting.

187

Numbers 1 to 5

Count the lily pads in the pond.
Color them in order.

Now color 5 fish friends for the frog to play with.

Note for parent: The numbers show your child how many objects (like lily pads) are in the set.

Writing Numbers 0 to 5

Start at the dot and follow the arrows to trace each number with a pencil. Read the number words.

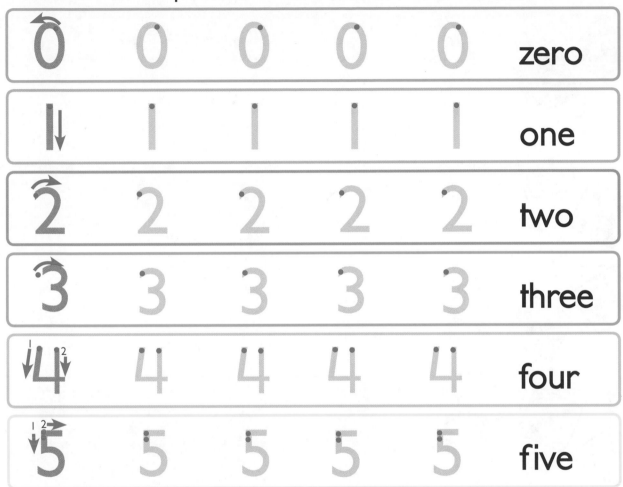

0 0 0 0 0	zero
1 1 1 1 1	one
2 2 2 2 2	two
3 3 3 3 3	three
4 4 4 4 4	four
5 5 5 5 5	five

Write the missing number in each box.

0 [ ] 2

1 [ ] 3

2 [ ] 4

3 [ ] 5

Note for parent: This activity demonstrates the correct formation of the numerals 0 to 5.

Numbers up to 10

Count the spots on the dice. Point to the numbers.
Trace them with your finger. Write the numbers.

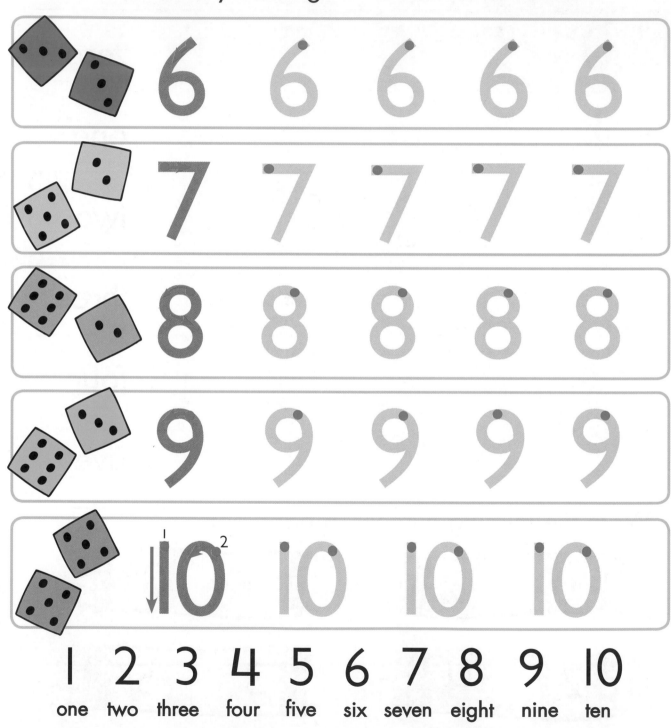

1	2	3	4	5	6	7	8	9	10
one	two	three	four	five	six	seven	eight	nine	ten

How Many?

Count the number of each thing and write the answers in the boxes.

ducklings

horse

flowers

bees

trees

pigs

sunflowers

cows

wheels

sheep

Color the picture.

Note for parent: This activity gives your child practice counting to 10. Ask your child to guess (estimate) how many of each thing first. Count to see how close they are.

191

Counting up to 10

Count the rabbits. Touch each rabbit as you count it.

Color a carrot for each rabbit.
How many carrots do you need?
Write the correct number in the box.

Point to each number as you count it.

| 1 | 2 | 3 | 4 | 5 | 6 | 7 | 8 | 9 | 10 |

Note for parent: Touching the objects as you count them reinforces the one-to-one relationship between the object and the number.

Writing Numbers 6 to 10

Start at the dot and follow the arrows to trace each number with a pencil. Read the number words.

6 6 6 6 6 6 6   six

7 7 7 7 7 7 7   seven

8 8 8 8 8 8 8   eight

9 9 9 9 9 9 9   nine

10 10 10 10 10   ten

Write the missing number in each box.

6 [ ] 8

7 [ ] 9

8 [ ] 10

Note for parent: This activity demonstrates the correct formation of the numerals 6 to 10.

193

Counting

Count the objects in the big picture.
Write the correct number in each box.

Comparing

Color most spaceships red. Color the rest of the spaceships blue. Write the numbers in the boxes.

☐ red spaceships

☐ blue spaceships

☐ red spaceships

☐ blue spaceships

☐ red spaceships

☐ blue spaceships

☐ spaceships all together

☐ red spaceships

☐ blue spaceships

☐ spaceships all together

Note for parent: Your child can choose the number of spaceships to color red, but there must be more red spaceships than blue ones.

195

Numbers and Counting

Write the numbers. Connect each picture to the right number. Connect each number to the right word.

four

one

two

five

three

Note for parent: Help your child to work with numbers by saying a number and asking them what number is one more/less.

197

Ordering Numbers up to 10

Draw lines to connect each train car to the next, in order from 1 to 10.

Note for parent: This activity provides practice in counting to 10 and the sequencing of numbers in the correct order.

Number 0 (zero)

Count the animals in each field.
Write the correct number in each box.

How many cows? ☐   How many sheep? ☐

How many lions? ☐   How many dogs? ☐

How many chickens? ☐   How many zebras? ☐

Note for parent: This activity helps to reinforce the concept of zero in a fun way.
Make up further silly questions to which the answer will be zero.

199

Counting On

Count on from the numbers in each row.
Write the missing number on each sail.

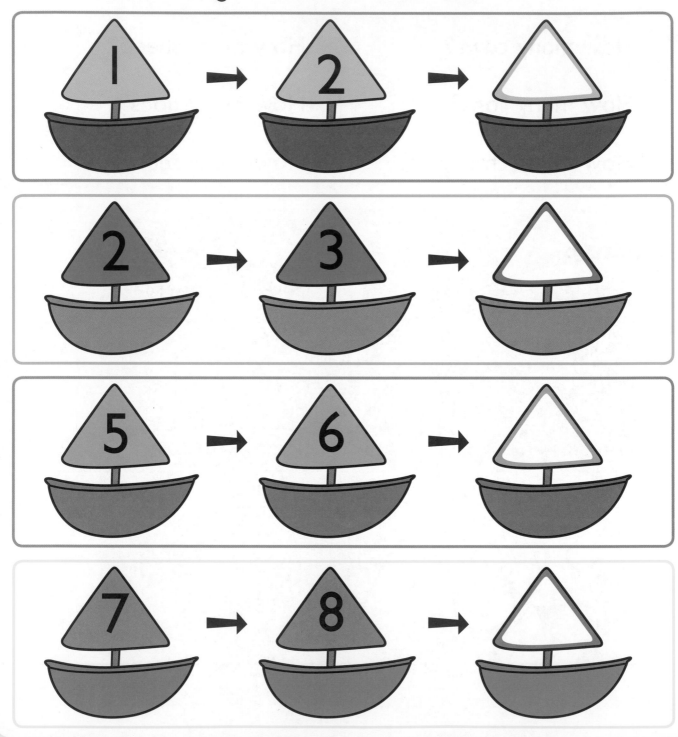

Note for parent: This activity provides practice in counting forwards from a number. Think of further examples using numbers up to 10.

Counting Back

Count back from the numbers in each row.
Write the missing number on each bus.

4 → 3 →

5 → 4 →

8 → 7 →

10 → 9 →

Note for parent: This activity provides practice in counting backward from a number. Play countdown games. Who will be first to finish? 5, 4, 3, 2, 1, go!

Counting

Count the spots on each dog.
Write the number in the box.

Connect the frogs that have
the same number of spots.

Note for parent: This activity gives practice in using counting skills in different ways.

Each frog needs 10 spots.
Draw in the missing spots.

Connect the pairs of dogs. Each pair must
have a total of 10 spots.

Note for parent: Help your child write down all the pairs of numbers that add up to 10.

203

Trace the numbers. Connect each kite to the right number. Connect each number to the right group of pictures at the bottom of each page.

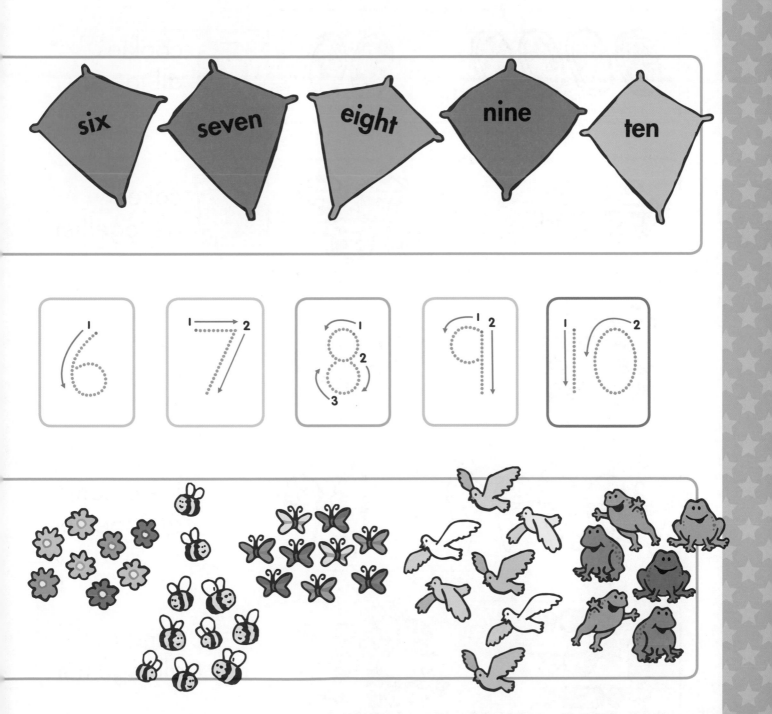

six seven eight nine ten

Note for parent: Help your child to work with numbers by saying a number and asking them what number is one more/less.

205

Putting Together

Count each set. Write how many there are all together.

cookies
all together

cakes
all together

pizzas
all together

ice creams
all together

candies
all together

Note for parent: Encourage your child to count on from the first number to find the total.

Count the spots on each monster.
How many spots are there all together?

☐ and ☐ make ☐ all together

☐ and ☐ make ☐ all together

☐ and ☐ make ☐ all together

Trace over the dotted lines to write **2**. The number **2** goes up, around and down, then across to the right.

 2 candles

2 bananas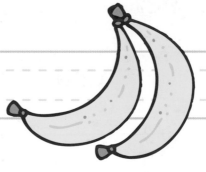

Write the number **2** on your own.

Note for parent: This activity groups 2, 3, and 5 together because they have a similar formation. The pencil moves up and down to form the numbers, ending in different directions.

Writing 3 and 5

Trace over the dotted lines to write **3**. The number **3** curves around to the middle, then around again.

3 3 3 3 3 3 3 3 3 3

3 cakes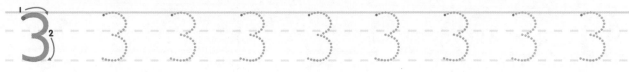

Write the number **3** on your own.

Trace over the dotted lines to write **5**. The number **5** goes down halfway, around, then straight across the top.

5 5 5 5 5 5 5 5 5 5

5 butterflies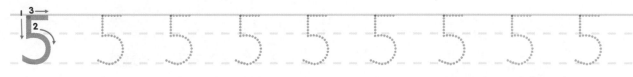

Write the number **5** on your own.

Writing 0 and 6

Trace over the dotted lines to write **0**. The number **0** curves to the left, then around again to join at the top.

0 0 0 0 0 0 0 0 0 0

0 to 60

Write the number **0** on your own.

Trace over the dotted lines to write **6**. The number **6** goes down, around, then joins in the middle.

6 6 6 6 6 6 6 6 6 6

6 cars

Write the number **6** on your own.

Writing 8 and 9

Trace over the dotted lines to write **8**. The number **8** curves around to the middle, then curves the other way.

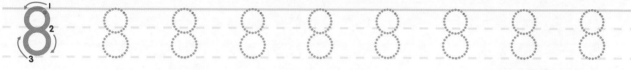

 **balloons**

Write the number **8** on your own.

Trace over the dotted lines to write **9**. The number **9** goes down halfway, then up to the top, and straight down again.

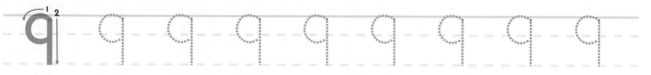

9 balloons

Write the number **9** on your own.

Writing 1 and 4

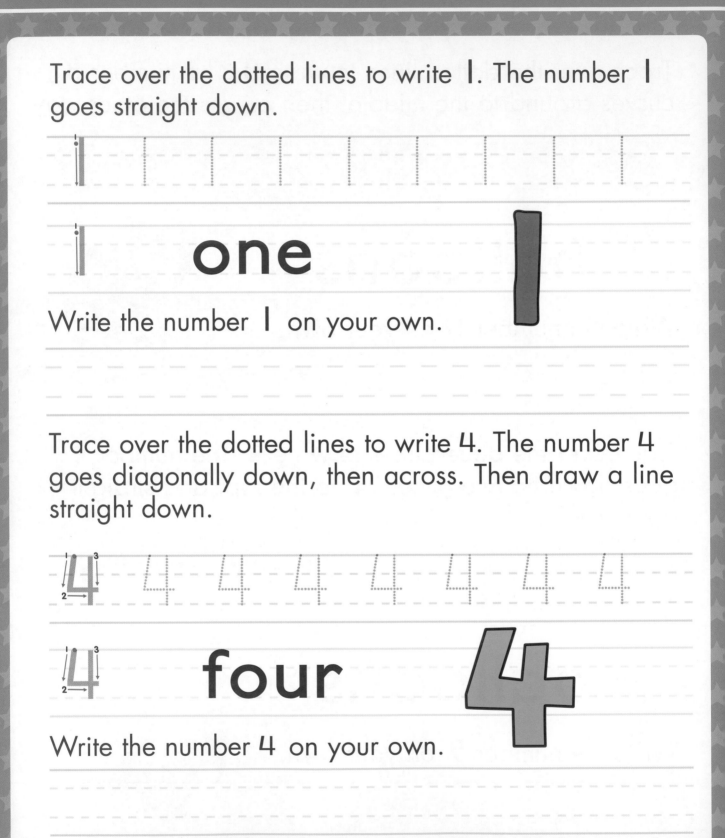

Trace over the dotted lines to write 1. The number 1 goes straight down.

Write the number 1 on your own.

one

Trace over the dotted lines to write 4. The number 4 goes diagonally down, then across. Then draw a line straight down.

four

Write the number 4 on your own.

Note for parent: Discuss with your child how, to complete number 4, the pencil must be lifted off the page.

Writing 7 and 10

Trace over the dotted lines to write **7**. The number **7** goes across, then diagonally down.

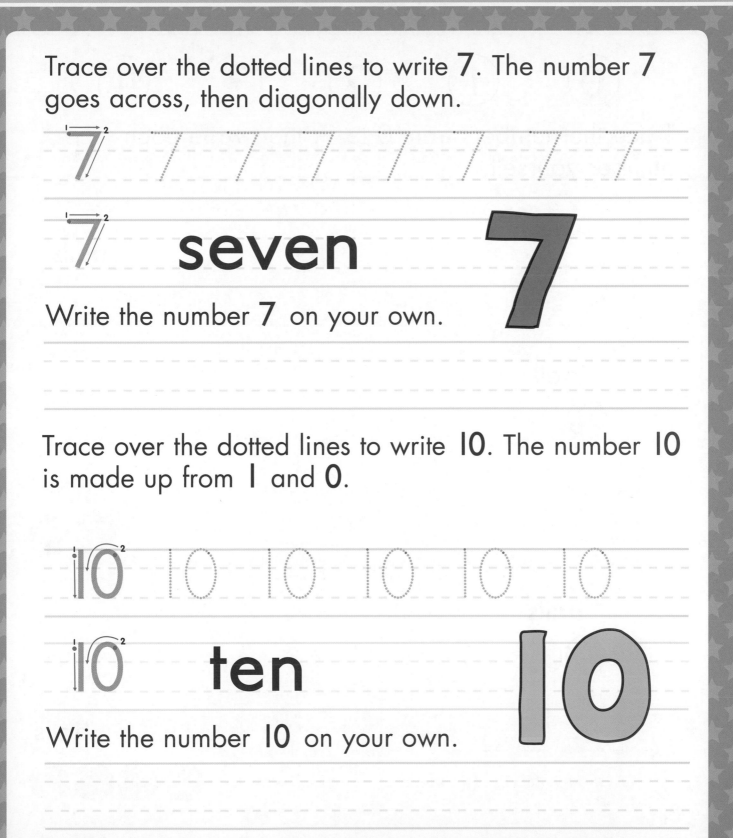

Write the number **7** on your own.

Trace over the dotted lines to write **10**. The number **10** is made up from **1** and **0**.

Write the number **10** on your own.

Note for parent: Show your child how to write the numbers 1 and 0 close together to make 10.

213

Numbers 0 to 9

(0) (1) (2) (3) (4)

Trace the numbers from 0 to 9, then write each number yourself.

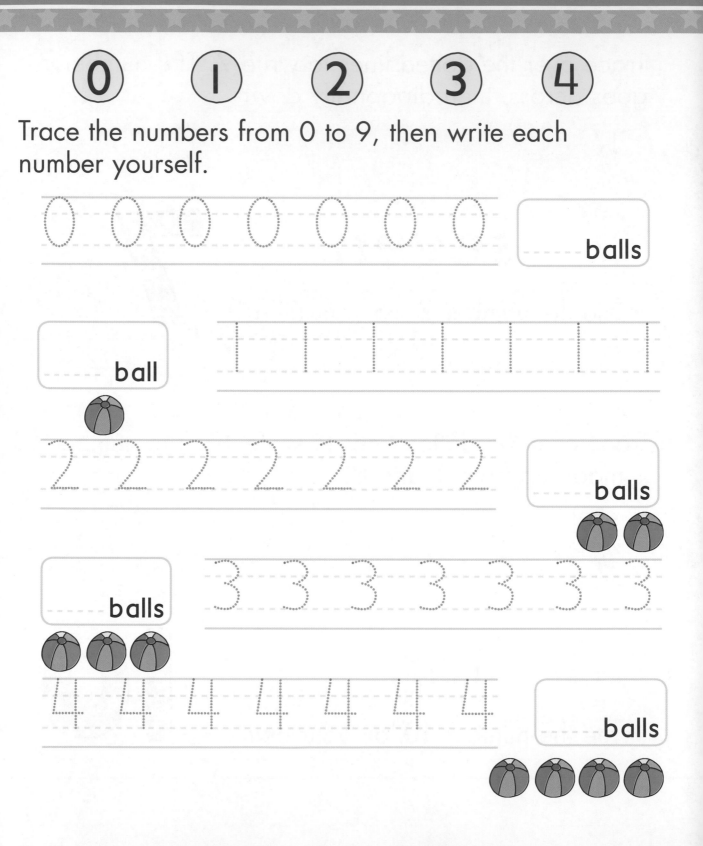

balls

ball

balls

balls

balls

Note for parent: Learning how to form numbers correctly is important. Encourage your child to form the numerals in a consistent size.

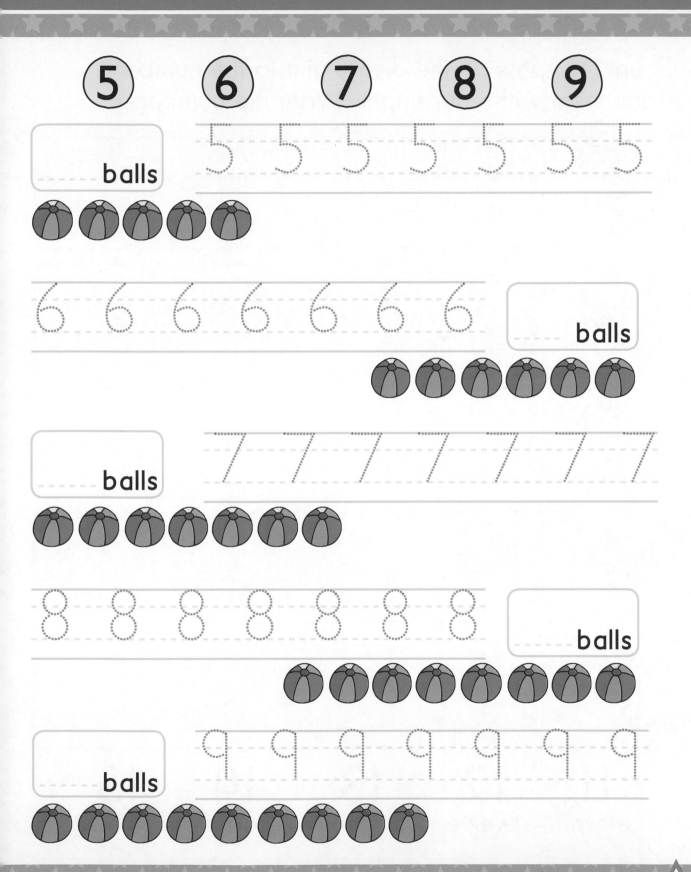

⑤ ⑥ ⑦ ⑧ ⑨

5 5 5 5 5 5 5 5

_ _ _ _ _ balls

6 6 6 6 6 6 6 6

_ _ _ _ _ balls

_ _ _ _ _ balls

7 7 7 7 7 7 7 7

8 8 8 8 8 8 8 8

_ _ _ _ _ balls

9 9 9 9 9 9 9 9

_ _ _ _ _ balls

Numbers up to 20

Count the spots on the dice. Point to the numbers.
Trace them with your finger. Write the numbers.

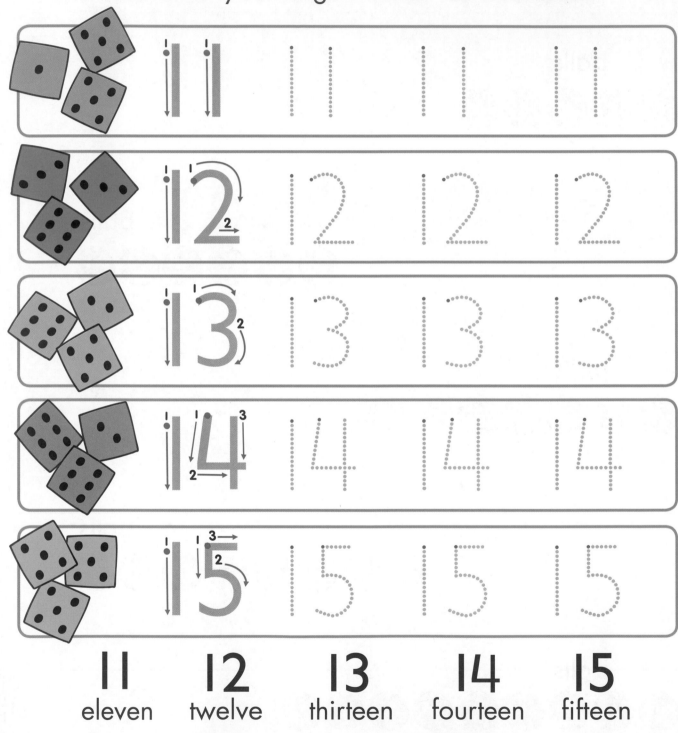

11 eleven **12** twelve **13** thirteen **14** fourteen **15** fifteen

16 sixteen **17** seventeen **18** eighteen **19** nineteen **20** twenty

Find and Count

Count how many there are of each colored snail.
Write the correct number in each box.

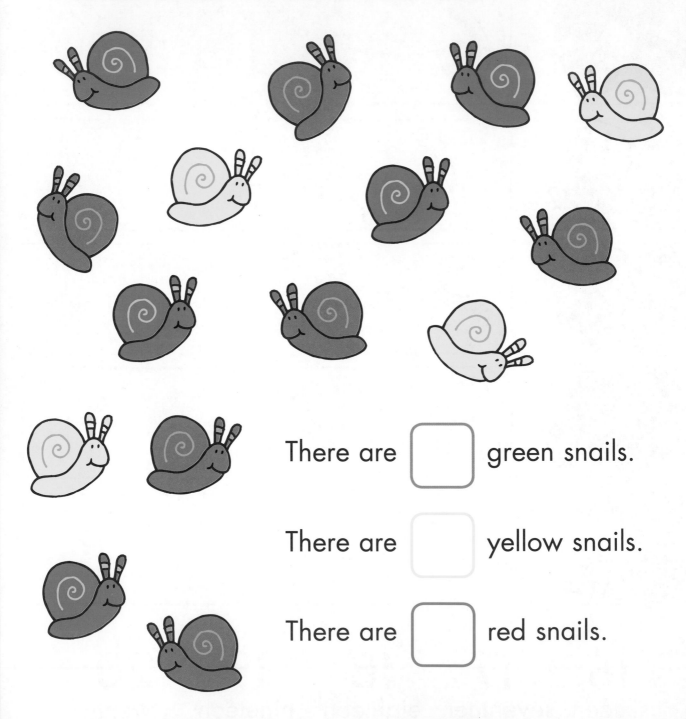

There are ☐ green snails.

There are ☐ yellow snails.

There are ☐ red snails.

Note for parent: Practice this activity using beads in three different colors.
Then ask your child to find out how many there are all together.

Counting up to 15

Count the butterflies. Touch each butterfly as you count it.

Color a flower for each butterfly. How many flowers do you need? Write the correct number in the box.

Point to each number as you count it.

1	2	3	4	5
6	7	8	9	10
11	12	13	14	15

Note for parent: This activity provides practice in counting to 15 and the sequencing of numbers in the correct order.

Emma and two of her friends are having a party.

How many drinks are there all together? ☐

Check the box if there are enough drinks for everyone to have **1** each. ☐

Note for parent: This activity introduces the concept of simple division—sharing something out so that each person has an equal amount.

How many cupcakes are there all together?

Check the box if there are enough cupcakes for everyone to have **2** each.

How many balloons are there all together?

Check the box if there are enough balloons for everyone to have **3** each.

Counting up to 20

Count the sheep. Draw a dot on each sheep as you count it.

Now read the numbers 1 to 20 out loud.

1	2	3	4	5	6	7	8	9	10
11	12	13	14	15	16	17	18	19	20

Note for parent: Drawing a dot on each sheep as you count it reinforces the one-to-one relationship between the object and the number.

Ordering Numbers up to 20

Draw lines to connect each duckling to the next, in order from 1 to **20**.

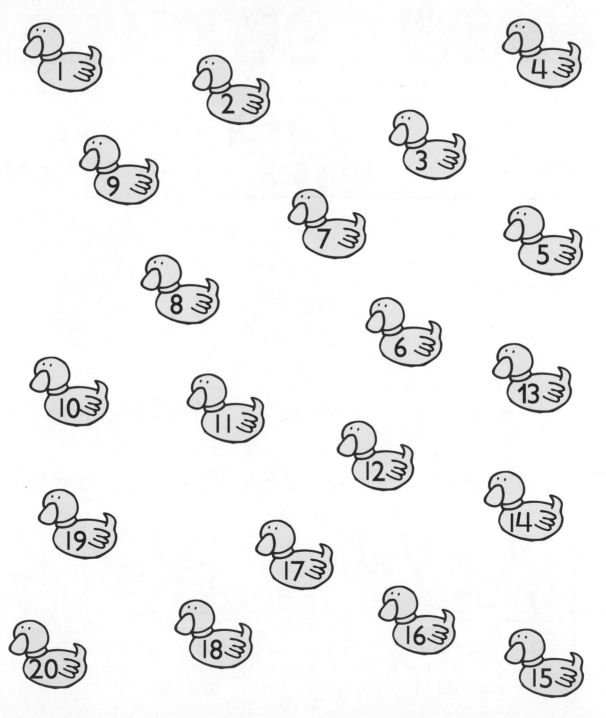

Note for parent: This activity provides practice in counting to 20 and the sequencing of numbers in the correct order.

Quick Quiz

Count each set. Write how many there are all together.

☐ cookies all together

☐ cakes all together

Count the spots on each monster.

☐ and ☐ make ☐ all together

Cross out two in each set. Write how many are left.

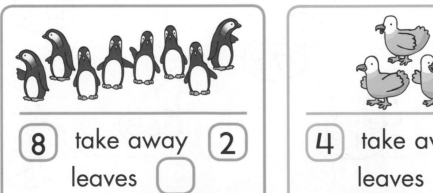

⑧ take away ② leaves ☐

④ take away ② leaves ☐

Numbers to 20

Connect each word to a number.

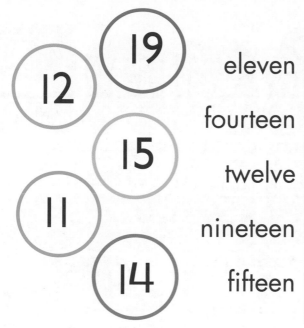

19	18
12	16
15	20
11	17
14	13

eleven | twenty

fourteen | sixteen

twelve | eighteen

nineteen | seventeen

fifteen | thirteen

Complete the number table.

eleven	11
	12
thirteen	
fourteen	
	15
sixteen	
	17
	18
nineteen	
	20

Group the numbers by their color circles above.

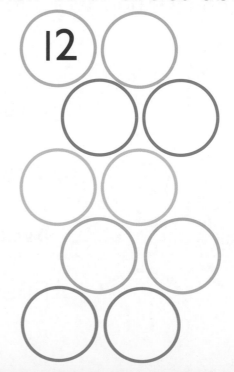

Note for parent: Solving problems using tables and sorting numbers using different criteria for grouping them are important math skills for your child at this age.

225

Counting to 20

Write in the missing numbers.

Connect each word to a number.

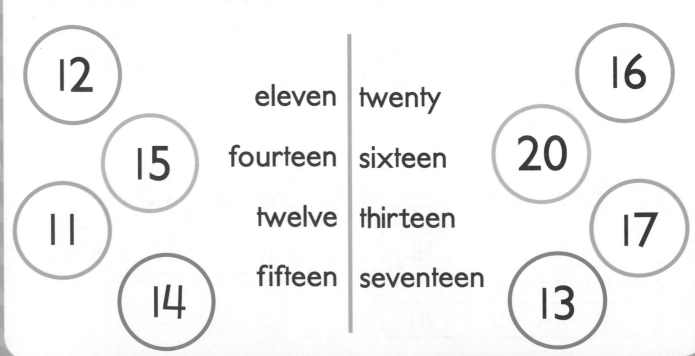

12			16
15	eleven	twenty	20
11	fourteen	sixteen	
	twelve	thirteen	17
14	fifteen	seventeen	13

Connect the Dots

Connect the dots in order.
Can you name the mystery animals?

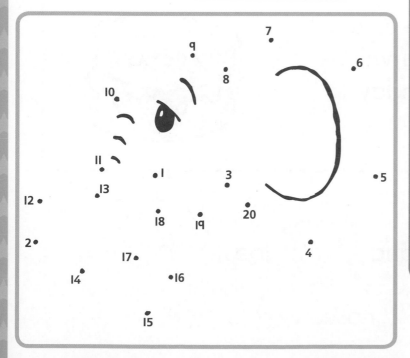

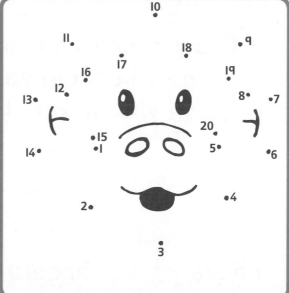

Note for parent: This activity gives further practice in counting to 20.

227

Counting Me

Write your first name on the dotted line.

....

Count the letters in your name.

There are [ ] letters in my name.

I am [ ]-years-old.

Draw candles on the cake to show how old you will be on your next birthday.

I have [ ] fingers and [ ] toes,

[ ] eyes and [ ] nose.

Note for parent: This activity encourages your child to use some of the numbers they have learned in a real context.

Draw a picture of yourself and your family here.

There are ☐ people in my family.

I can count up to ☐ .

Math

Helping Your Child

- The activities in this section will help your child learn about math. Pictures provide hints and clues to support their understanding.

- Your child will gain the confidence to: compare numbers, attempt addition and subtraction sums, count forward and backward.

- Your child will learn about: adding and taking away, finding differences, and shapes.

- Set aside time to do the activities together. Do a little at a time so that your child enjoys learning.

- Give lots of encouragement and praise.

- The answers are on pages 316—320.

Contents

Pretty Patterns

Color the clothes on the lines to make patterns.

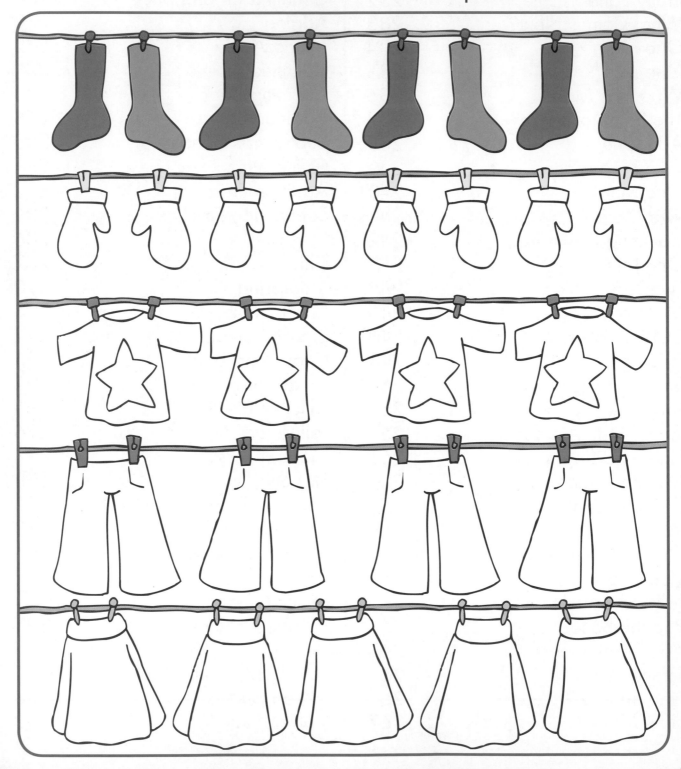

Note for parent: Use beads, toy bricks, or other objects to make up sequences based on color, size, or shape.

What Comes Next?

Draw the right shapes to continue the patterns.
Color the shapes.

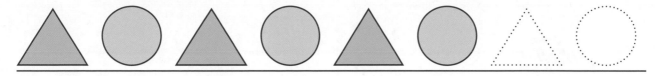

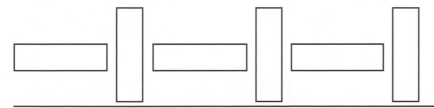

Note for parent: Encourage your child to draw shape patterns of their own on blank paper.
Use different colors to create different patterns as well.

233

One More

Draw 1 more. Count the objects. How many are there all together? Write the numbers in the boxes.

draw 1 more   3

draw 1 more

draw 1 more

draw 1 more

Note for parent: This page prepares your child for adding. Ask How many all together? Three spiders and one more spider makes four spiders all together.

One Less

Circle the correct answers.

 One helicopter flies away.
How many are left?

3
2
1

 One mouse runs away.
How many are left?

3
5
4

One butterfly flies away.
How many are left?

2
3
4

 One car drives away.
How many are left?

1
2
3

Note for parent: This page prepares your child for subtracting or taking away. Play a game: show five fingers, hide one finger to show one less. How many fingers are left?

Who Has More?

Look at the pictures. Check the person in each row who has more.

Note for parent: This activity gives more practice in counting from 1 to 3.

The Same or More?

Connect each rabbit to a hole. Are there more rabbits or more holes? Check the correct box.

more rabbits ☐ more holes ☐

Connect each kennel to a dog. Are there more dogs or more houses? Check the correct box.

more kennels ☐ more dogs ☐

Note for parent: Matching objects one by one shows if the numbers are the same or different.

Add One

Point to each picture and count the objects.
Say the numbers out loud.
Write the totals in the boxes.

1 + 1 = **2**

2 + 1 =

3 + 1 =

Note for parent: Counting on shows that the last number counted gives the total. Hold up two fingers, then hold up one more. Two fingers plus one finger makes three fingers all together.

Take Away One

Count the animals. Take one away.
How many are left?
Write in the missing numbers.

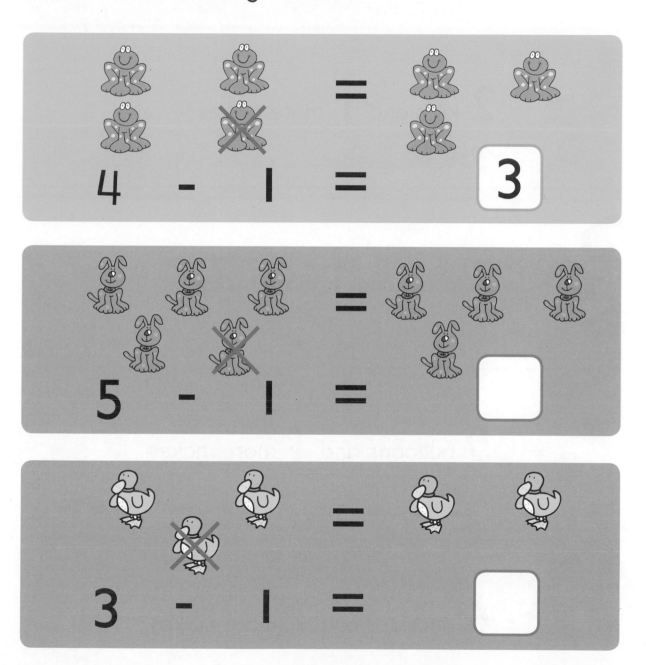

4 - 1 = 3

5 - 1 =

3 - 1 =

One More

Draw one more object in each row. Count how many objects there are all together. Write the correct number in each box.

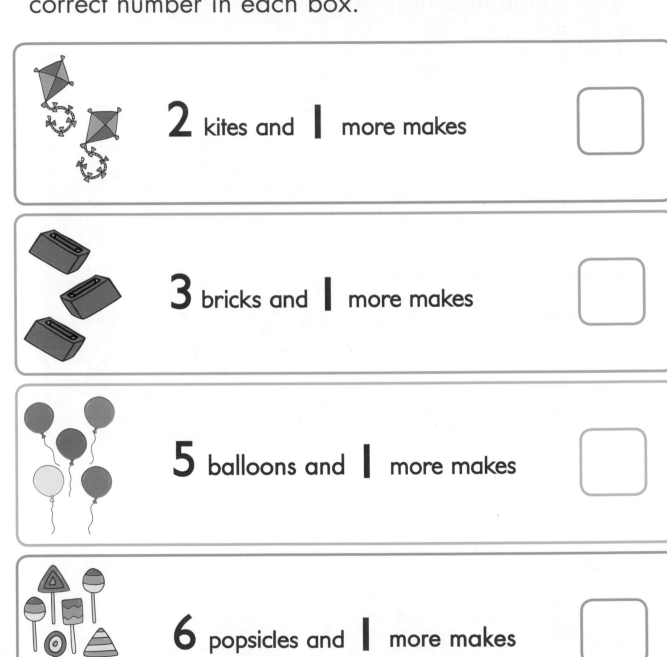

2 kites and **1** more makes

3 bricks and **1** more makes

5 balloons and **1** more makes

6 popsicles and **1** more makes

Note for parent: This activity introduces the concept of addition by drawing one more. You can practice the addition of one more using groups of counting beads or buttons.

Two More

Count how many bananas there are all together in each row. Write the correct number in each box.

 **1** banana and **2** more makes **3**

 **2** bananas and **2** more makes

 **3** bananas and **2** more makes

 **4** bananas and **2** more makes

5 bananas and **2** more makes

Note for parent: When your child has grasped adding two more, try adding three more—use counting beads or buttons.

241

Have fun counting and singing this song.

5 fat sausages sizzling in a pan,
All of a sudden, one went BANG!

4 fat sausages sizzling in a pan,
All of a sudden, one went BANG!

3 fat sausages sizzling in a pan,
All of a sudden, one went BANG!

2 fat sausages sizzling in a pan,
All of a sudden, one went BANG!

1 fat sausage sizzling in a pan,
All of a sudden, one went BANG!

No fat sausages sizzling in a pan!

Note for parent: Singing songs that have a counting element is a good way to reinforce number skills. Extend to larger numbers with Ten green bottles and Ten in the bed.

One Less

Cross out one sweet treat on each plate.
Count how many are left on each plate.
Write the correct number in each box.

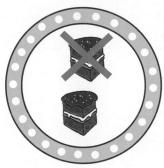 **2** take away **1** leaves 1

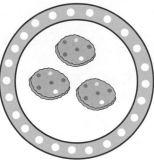 **3** take away **1** leaves

 **5** take away **1** leaves

 **7** take away **1** leaves

 **8** take away **1** leaves

Two Less

Cross out two pieces of fruit on each plate.
Count how many are left on each plate.
Write the correct number in each box.

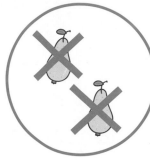 **2** take away **2** leaves `0`

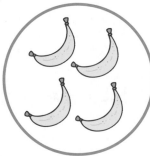 **4** take away **2** leaves

 **5** take away **2** leaves

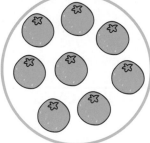 **8** take away **2** leaves

 **9** take away **2** leaves

Note for parent: Show your child what subtraction means in a familiar context. For example, after a meal you might say: We had four bowls of ice cream—now there are none left!

More or Less?

Who has more apples—Teddy or Robot? Guess first, then count. Write the correct number in each box.

Teddy has [ ] apples.   Robot has [ ] apples.

Who has fewer oranges—Tom or Rob? Guess first, then count. Write the correct number in each box.

Tom has [ ] oranges.   Rob has [ ] oranges.

Starting to Add

Write in the missing numbers.

 _____ and _____ make ☐ all together

 _____ and _____ make ☐ all together

 _____ +  _____ = ◯   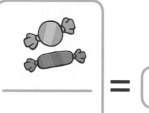 _____ +  _____ = ◯

 _____ +  _____ = ◯    _____ +  _____ = ◯

Note for parent: In this activity your child is adding with objects, which helps to prepare them for adding with numbers.

Draw the missing socks above each arrow.

1 + 4 = 5

2 + 3 = 5

3 + 4 = 7

4 + 3 = 7

Write the missing numbers.

$\boxed{}$ + 5 = 8

$\boxed{}$ + 4 = 8

$\boxed{}$ + 5 = 6

$\boxed{}$ + 5 = 7

Adding

Draw in the extra crayons.
Write the total number of crayons.

1 add 4	1 + 4 =
 3 add 3	3 + 3 =
 4 add 6	4 + 6 =

There should be 10 cherries on each plate.
Draw the missing cherries.

4 +   = 10

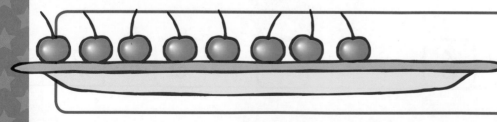

8 +   = 10

Note for parent: Your child may need to use the number line on page 249
to complete these additions.

Use the number line above to help you.
Write how many beads are on each necklace.

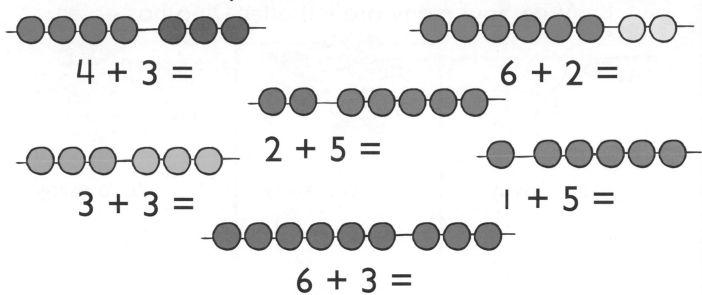

4 + 3 =

6 + 2 =

2 + 5 =

3 + 3 =

1 + 5 =

6 + 3 =

Connect the scarves that have the same total.

1 + 5

8 + 2

5 + 2

4 + 6

4 + 3

3 + 1

2 + 2

3 + 3

Starting to Take Away

Dino the dinosaur eats 2 of everything he sees.
Cross out how many pieces of food Dino eats.
Write how many are left after Dino has eaten.

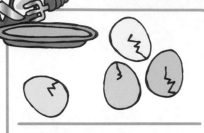 [ ] take away
2 leaves [ ]

 [ ] take away
2 leaves [ ]

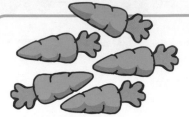 [ ] take away
2 leaves [ ]

 [ ] take away
2 leaves [ ]

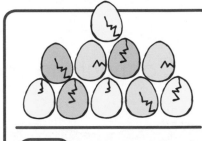 [ ] take away
2 leaves [ ]

 [ ] take away
2 leaves [ ]

3 − 2 = [ ]

2 − 2 = [ ]

9 − 2 = [ ]

Note for parent: Taking away is a first step toward learning about subtraction.

How many fish has Charlie the cat eaten from each bowl? Connect each START bowl to the correct FINISH bowl.

START

FINISH

take away 2

take away 1

take away 2

take away 2

take away 3

take away 6

Taking Away

Cross off the animals to be taken away.
Write how many are left.

4 take away 2

$4 - 2 =$

7 take away 3

$7 - 3 =$

8 take away 5

$8 - 5 =$

Only 3 rockets are needed. Cross off the ones that have to be taken away. Write the answer.

$5 - \quad = 3$

$7 - \quad = 3$

Note for parent: Your child may need to use the number track on page 253 to complete these subtractions.

Use the number line above to help you answer the subtractions.

4 – 1 =

5 – 3 =

8 – 7 =

5 – 5 =

9 – 5 =

10 – 2 =

Connect the stars that have the same answer.

10 – 5

8 – 7

5 – 0

10 – 7

6 – 3

6 – 5

How Many Are Left?

Cross out two in each set. Write how many are left.

5 take away 2

leaves ☐

6 take away 2

leaves ☐

8 take away 2

leaves ☐

4 take away 2

leaves ☐

Some birds are flying away.
How many are left on the branch?

9 take away 3 leaves ☐

Note for parent: This activity will help your child begin to understand the idea of taking away (subtracting).

Finding Differences

How many more children are there than chairs?

☐ children

☐ chairs

difference → ☐

☐ children

☐ chairs

difference → ☐

☐ children

☐ chairs

difference → ☐

Note for parent: Finding the difference is the same as counting up from the smaller number to the larger one.

Number Machines

Candies go into these adding machines.
Write how many come out of each machine.

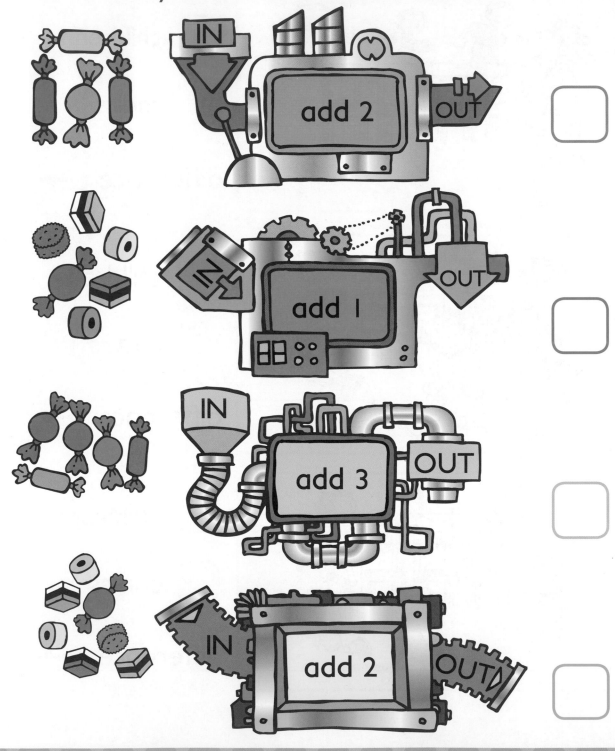

Note for parent: Encourage your child to count on from the IN number for adding, and to count back for taking away.

Drinks go into these take-away machines.
Write how many come out of each machine.

Hidden Numbers

There are **9** ducks in each line, but some are hidden. Write down how many are hidden.

2

Note for parent: These are good activities to do with real toys. Make them fun!

What's the Total?

Count the different crayons. How many are there in each jar? Write down the totals.

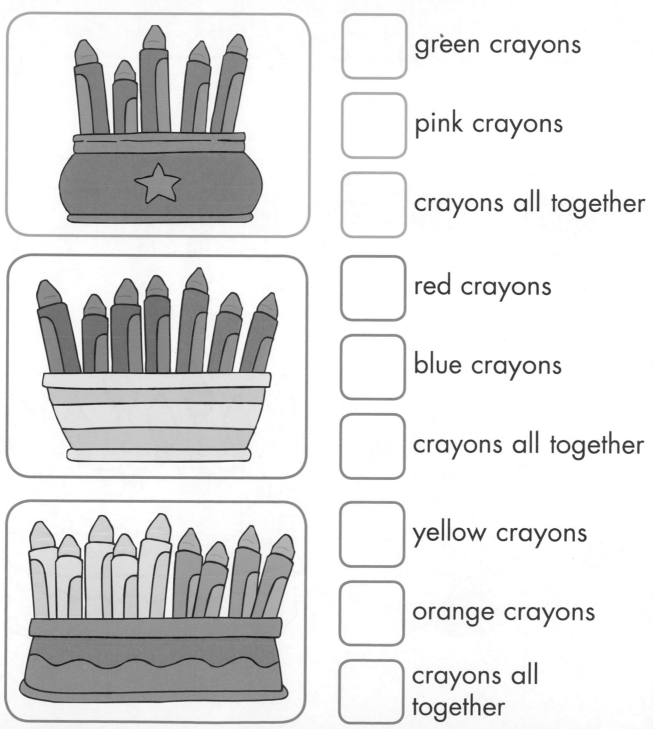

☐ green crayons

☐ pink crayons

☐ crayons all together

☐ red crayons

☐ blue crayons

☐ crayons all together

☐ yellow crayons

☐ orange crayons

☐ crayons all together

Ordering Numbers

Write in the missing numbers.

Note for parent: This activity gives your child practice in counting forward and backward. Play countdown games. Who will be first to finish? 5, 4, 3, 2, 1, go!

Write the totals in the boxes.
There are two spots all together.

2

Draw two arms on each teddy.
How many arms all together?

Draw two legs on each duck.
How many legs all together?

Draw two ears on each cat.
How many ears all together?

Note for parent: This activity gives your child practice in counting in twos up to ten. Put 10 counters in groups of two. Point and count to each group—2, 4, 6, 8, 10.

261

Cross out four animals from each set.
Write how many are left.

$$6 - 4 = \boxed{}$$

$$5 - 4 = \boxed{}$$

$$8 - 4 = \boxed{}$$

$$7 - 4 = \boxed{}$$

Note for parent: These activities will help your child to recognize the symbol for subtraction.

Pop the Balloons

Pop four balloons from each bunch by crossing them out. Write how many are left.

9 – 4 = ☐

10 – 4 = ☐

4 – 4 = ☐

Note for parent: Your child should begin to use the zero symbol, 0, for none or nothing.

Adding Numbers

Look at the sums. Then use a number line to find the answers. Write in the answers.

$1 + 2 =$ **3** The frog starts on number 1. He makes two jumps forward and lands on number 3.

| 1 | 2 | 3 | 4 | 5 | 6 | 7 | 8 | 9 | 10 |

$2 + 3 =$ ☐

| 1 | 2 | 3 | 4 | 5 | 6 | 7 | 8 | 9 | 10 |

$4 + 4 =$ ☐

| 1 | 2 | 3 | 4 | 5 | 6 | 7 | 8 | 9 | 10 |

$5 + 4 =$ ☐

| 1 | 2 | 3 | 4 | 5 | 6 | 7 | 8 | 9 | 10 |

Note for parent: This activity shows your child how to use a number line to add. Start at a number and add on another number without beginning from 1 each time.

Taking Away

Look at the sums. Then use a number line to find the answers. Write in the answers.

3 − 2 = | 1 |

The frog starts on number 3. He makes two jumps backward and lands on number 1.

1 2 3 4 5 6 7 8 9 10

5 − 2 = | |

1 2 3 4 5 6 7 8 9 10

7 − 4 = | |

1 2 3 4 5 6 7 8 9 10

10 − 3 = | |

1 2 3 4 5 6 7 8 9 10

Note for parent: This activity shows how to take away (subtract) using a number line. Explain that taking something away means you end up with less.

Hop up to 20

Draw a line to join each frog to a lily pad so that the number and dots add up to **20**.

Note for parent: This will teach your child some number bonds up to 20, in multiples of 5. These simple addition facts make adding and multiplying much easier.

How Many?

How many marbles in each jar? Make a guess.
Count to see if you are right. Draw more marbles
in each jar to make 20.

guess

count

guess

count

guess

count

guess

count

Note for parent: This activity gives practice in estimating. Ask questions such as Do you think there are more than 10? Do you think there are less than 20?

Counting on and Back

Use the number line to help you count on.
Connect each monster to its correct answer on the line.

8 + 3

9 + 5

8 + 7

6 + 7

9 + 9

6 + 4

0 1 2 3 4 5 6 7 8 9 10 11 12 13 14 15 16 17 18 19 20

10 + 3

10 + 5

10 + 8

12 + 6

10 + 10

15 + 1

Note for parent: This activity will help your child to use a number line to count on and back. Encourage your child to count on in twos and fives along the number line.

Use the number line to help you count back. Connect each spaceship to its correct answer on the line.

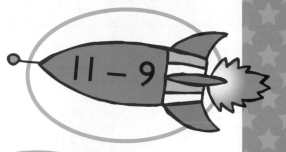

0 1 2 3 4 5 6 7 8 9 10 11 12 13 14 15 16 17 18 19 20

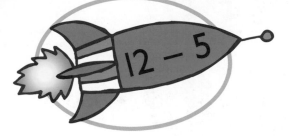

Note for parent: Encourage your child to count back in twos and fives along the number line.

269

Adding

Draw the extra balloons in each row.
Write the correct totals.

 2 add 3   2 + 3 = ☐

 3 add 4   3 + 4 = ☐

 4 add 5   4 + 5 = ☐

Write how many there are all together.

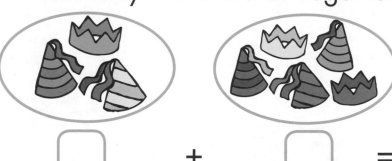

☐ + ☐ = ☐

☐ + ☐ = ☐

Note for parent: Ask your child what the addition sign (+) and the equals sign (=) mean. This will help them recognize and use the signs correctly.

Write how many colored pencils there are all together.

 3 + 2 = ☐

 2 + 2 = ☐

 4 + 3 = ☐

 5 + 1 = ☐

 6 + 3 = ☐

 4 + 5 = ☐

Connect each sum to the correct total.

5 + 2   3 + 3   4 + 1   1 + 3   4 + 4

5   8   6   7   4

Taking Away

Two children get out of each of these trains.
How many are left on each train?

7 take away 2 is   7 – 2 =

5 take away 2 is   5 – 2 =

8 take away 2 is   8 – 2 =

Cross out some flags. Write how many are left.

9 – is

Note for parent: Use the words subtract and take away with your child to help them recognize and understand the subtraction sign (−).

Draw how many balls come out of the machines.
Write the totals in the colored boxes.

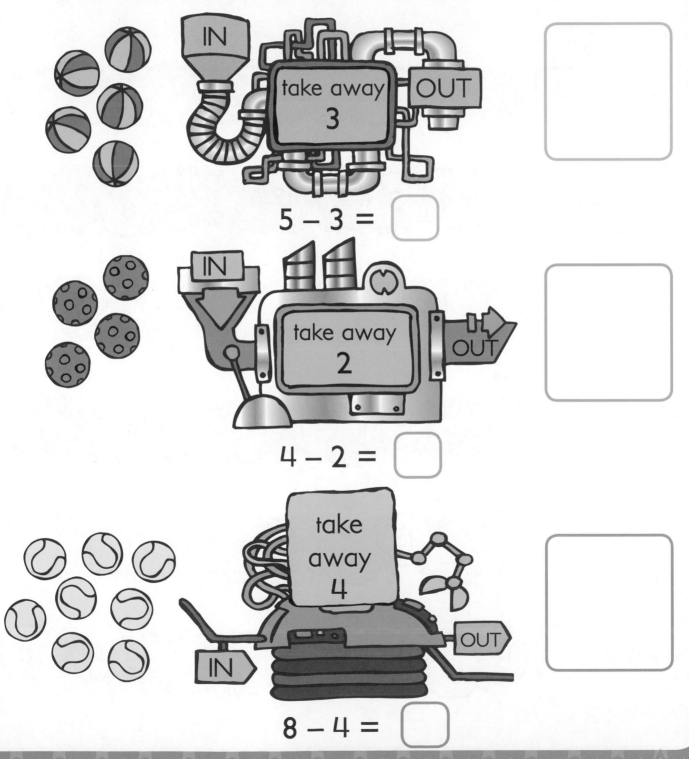

5 − 3 =

4 − 2 =

8 − 4 =

Counting on

Use the number line to count on. Show the jumps and write the answer. The first one has been done for you.

$4 + 2 = \boxed{6}$

1 2 3 4 5 6 7 8 9 10

$5 + 4 = \boxed{}$

1 2 3 4 5 6 7 8 9 10

$7 + 3 = \boxed{}$

1 2 3 4 5 6 7 8 9 10

$11 + 2 = \boxed{}$

11 12 13 14 15 16 17 18 19 20

$14 + 5 = \boxed{}$

11 12 13 14 15 16 17 18 19 20

$13 + 7 = \boxed{}$

11 12 13 14 15 16 17 18 19 20

Note for parent: This activity introduces adding two-digit numbers. Encourage your child to count on in twos and fives along each number line.

Connect each rocket to the correct answer on the number line.

1 2 3 4 5 6 7 8 9 10

5 + 2 =

3 + 3 =

3 + 1 =

4 + 1 =

6 + 3 =

Write the missing numbers in these counting patterns.

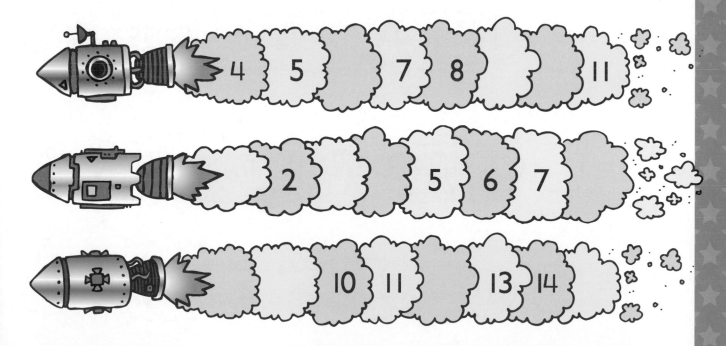

4 5   7 8   11

   2   5 6 7

      10 11   13 14

Counting Back

Use the number line to count back. Show the jumps and write the answer.

6 − 3 = ☐

1 2 3 4 5 6 7 8 9 10

5 − 2 = ☐

1 2 3 4 5 6 7 8 9 10

8 − 4 = ☐

1 2 3 4 5 6 7 8 9 10

13 − 1 = ☐

11 12 13 14 15 16 17 18 19 20

16 − 3 = ☐

11 12 13 14 15 16 17 18 19 20

17 − 6 = ☐

11 12 13 14 15 16 17 18 19 20

Note for parent: This activity introduces subtracting from two-digit numbers. Encourage your child to count back in twos and fives along each number line.

Work out each answer. Color the correct number in the number line to match.

Addition Bonds

Make these totals in different ways.
Write the answers in the boxes.

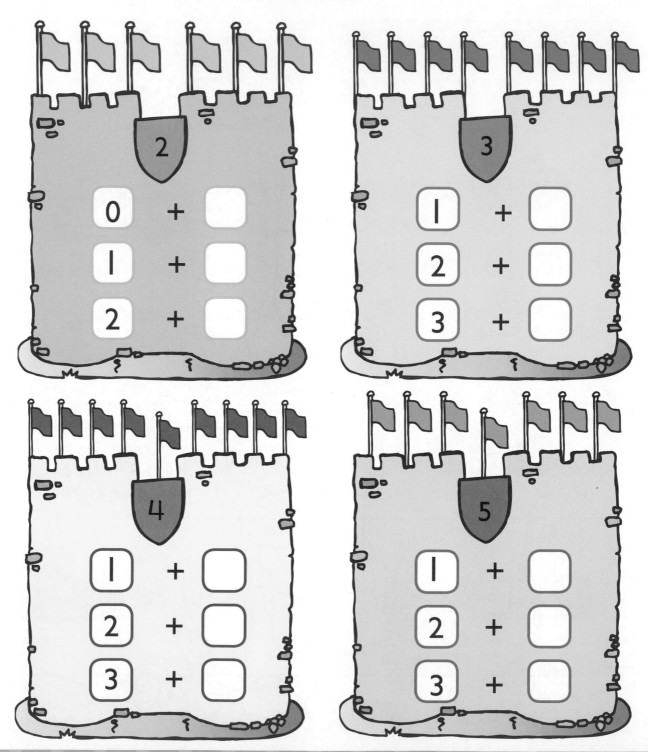

2

0 + ☐

1 + ☐

2 + ☐

3

1 + ☐

2 + ☐

3 + ☐

4

1 + ☐

2 + ☐

3 + ☐

5

1 + ☐

2 + ☐

3 + ☐

Draw a line from each flower to the pot with the correct total.

What can you see if you color all the shapes with a total of 10?

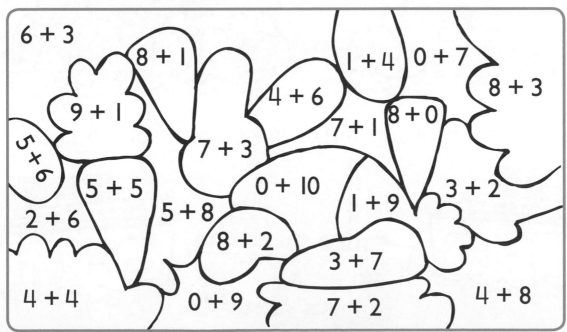

Subtraction Bonds

Find different ways of making 1 and 2.

Lighthouse 1:
2 – ☐
3 – ☐
4 – ☐
5 – ☐
10 – ☐

Lighthouse 2:
5 – ☐
4 – ☐
3 – ☐
2 – ☐
10 – ☐

Find different ways to make the answer of ⑤.

☐ – ☐

☐ – ☐

☐ – ☐

Note for parent: Subtraction bonds with totals up to five bond pairs with a total of ten are key learning objectives for your child in this age group.

Connect the sums to the correct totals.

5 + 2   4 + 1   4 + 4

5   8   7

Draw how many balls come out of the machines.

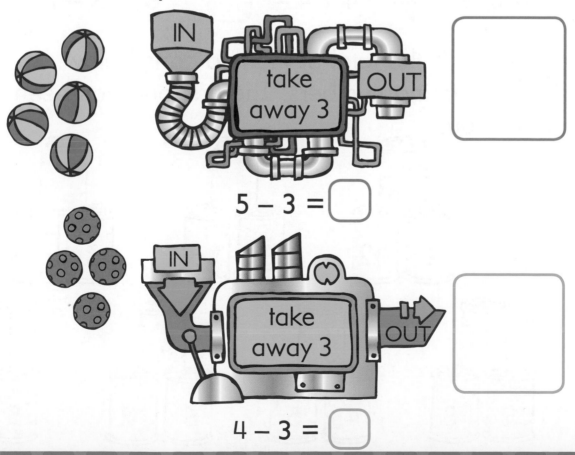

IN   take away 3   OUT

5 − 3 =

IN   take away 3   OUT

4 − 3 =

Addition Practice

Write the answers in the boxes. Use the number line to help you.

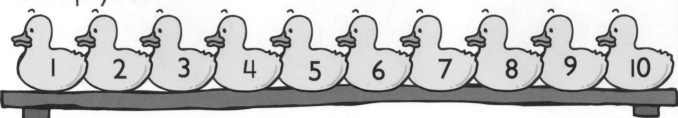

4 + 3 = ☐   6 + 2 = ☐   5 + 5 = ☐

9 + 1 = ☐   7 + 2 = ☐   3 + 5 = ☐

2 + 4 = ☐   4 + 4 = ☐   6 + 3 = ☐

The top can is the total of the two cans below. Write the missing numbers. The first one has been done for you.

Note for parent: On a separate piece of paper, ask your child to write out the addition facts shown on the tin cans as sums using the + and = symbols they have learned.

Write the missing numbers.

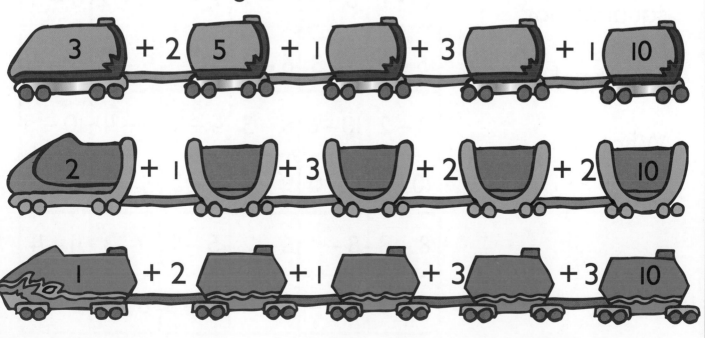

+ 2 = 4

+ 3 = 6

4 + = 8

5 + = 10

+ 8 = 10

6 + = 10

+ 7 = 10

1 + = 10

+ 0 = 10

Follow these trails to reach 10.
Write the missing totals.

3 + 2 5 + 1 + 3 + 1 10

2 + 1 + 3 + 2 + 2 10

1 + 2 + 1 + 3 + 3 10

Subtraction Practice

Write the answers in the boxes. Use the number line to help you.

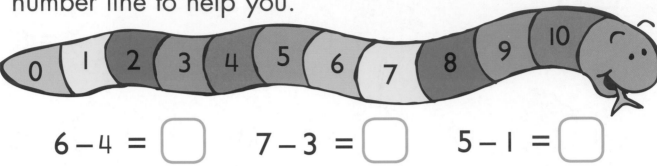

6 − 4 = ☐   7 − 3 = ☐   5 − 1 = ☐

8 − 5 = ☐   6 − 3 = ☐   9 − 4 = ☐

10 − 5 = ☐   7 − 4 = ☐   8 − 3 = ☐

Color the squares that have an answer of 4.

What can you see?

6 − 1	5 − 1	7 − 2	7 − 4	8 − 2	8 − 3
5 − 2	7 − 3	6 − 3	10 − 1	9 − 7	5 − 4
3 − 2	10 − 6	8 − 5	4 − 4	6 − 4	10 − 5
10 − 7	4 − 0	9 − 6	9 − 5	5 − 0	6 − 5
8 − 3	8 − 4	6 − 2	5 − 1	7 − 3	4 − 4
5 − 3	9 − 4	7 − 1	10 − 6	8 − 6	3 − 0

Note for parent: On a separate piece of paper, ask your child to write out the subtractions shown in the squares and include the answers using the − and = symbols they have learned.

Write the missing numbers.

⬡ − 5 = 5   △ − 4 = 4   ⬤ − 3 = 3

4 − ⬡ = 2   10 − ⯃ = 4   10 − ▢ = 8

▯ − 3 = 7   ⬯ − 8 = 2   10 − ✶ = 1

Solve each problem as you go. Write the total in each star. Connect each pair of stars with the same answer.

4 − 3

8 − 5

9 − 7

10 − 3

9 − 2

7 − 4

6 − 4

7 − 6

285

Money

How much? Add up the money in each purse.

total = ☐

total = ☐

total = ☐

total = ☐

Circle the items you would buy. They must add up to 20.

pencil

apple

banana

cake

marble

ice cream

Note for parent: This activity gives additional practice in adding up to 20. Use real coins to match the money in each purse—this will help your child to count out and add them up.

Time

Fill in the missing numbers.

What time is it?

It is [ ] o'clock.

It is [ ] o'clock   It is [ ] o'clock   It is [ ] o'clock

It is [ ] o'clock   It is [ ] o'clock   It is [ ] o'clock

Note for parent: Time can be a tricky concept for children. Encourage your child to read the clock at set times each day, such as breakfast at 8 o'clock, lunch at 12 o'clock, etc.

Time

Write in the missing numbers on the clock.

Write the times under each clock.

.... o'clock

.... o'clock

.... o'clock

Look at the times. Draw in the missing hands.

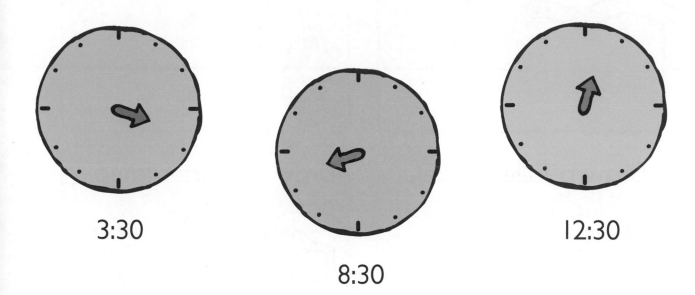

3:30

8:30

12:30

Write the times under each clock.

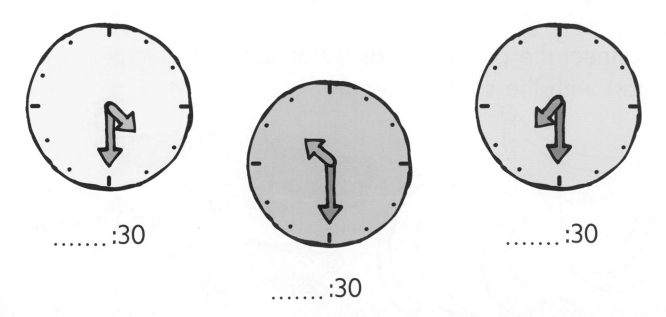

.......:30

.......:30

.......:30

Note for parent: For further practice with the concept of time, ask your child if they can name the days of the week and the months of the year.

289

Measuring

Draw a longer worm.

Draw a bigger flower.

Draw a taller rocket.

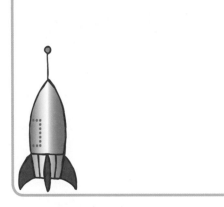

Draw a shorter lamp post.

Connect the pictures in order of size.
Start with the smallest.

Note for parent: In this activity your child is learning to estimate and compare measurements.

Quick Quiz

Use the number line to help you write the answers.

0 1 2 3 4 5 6 7 8 9 10

$2 + 4 =$

$3 + 3 =$

$5 + 4 =$

$6 + 4 =$

$5 + 5 =$

$2 + 3 =$

$1 + 7 =$

$2 + 7 =$

$2 + 2 =$

$10 - 1 =$

$5 - 3 =$

$4 - 2 =$

$8 - 3 =$

$6 - 5 =$

$10 - 6 =$

$7 - 4 =$

$9 - 6 =$

$7 - 2 =$

Note for parent: Encourage children to look back through the book if they need help with the answers.

291

Big and Small

Check the big animal.

Draw the small animal.

Check the small cake.

Draw the big cake.

Note for parent: This activity helps your child compare sizes. Use words such as small, smaller, smallest, big, bigger, biggest.

Heavy and Light

heavy   **light**

light   **heavy**

Check the heavy animal.

Draw the light animal.

Check the light object.

Draw the heavy object.

Note for parent: This activity helps your child compare different weights. Use words such as light, lighter, lightest, heavy, heavier, heaviest.

Longer or Shorter?

Look at this pencil.

Find all the pencils that are longer than this one.
Circle them.

What color is the longest pencil? What color
is the shortest pencil?

Note for parent: This activity helps your child to compare objects. Ask them to explain how they found the answer.

Taller or Shorter?

Draw a taller tree. Draw a shorter tree.

Draw a shorter house. Draw a taller house.

Draw a circle around the shortest child.

Note for parent: This activity gives your child practice in identifying short and tall. Use words such as short, shorter, shortest, tall, taller, tallest.

295

Tall, Short, and Long

 **tall**

 **long**

 **short**

Circle the shortest animal.

Circle the tallest house.

Draw a scarf longer than this one.

Note for parent: Measure the height of your child and other family members. Compare them using words such as tall, taller, tallest, short, shorter, shortest.

More or Less?

Circle the cake with more candles.

Circle the ladybug with less spots.

Which boxes have more in them? Check the one you think has more. Then count to see if you are right.

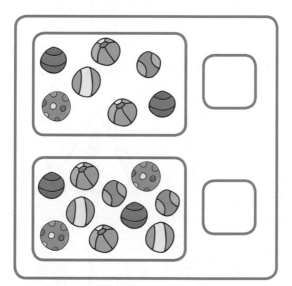 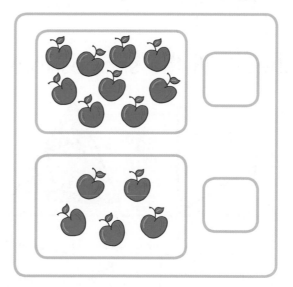

Draw a nest with more birds in it than this one.

Note for parent: This activity helps your child to understand estimating and the terms more and less.

Flat Shapes

Cross the odd one out in each ring.

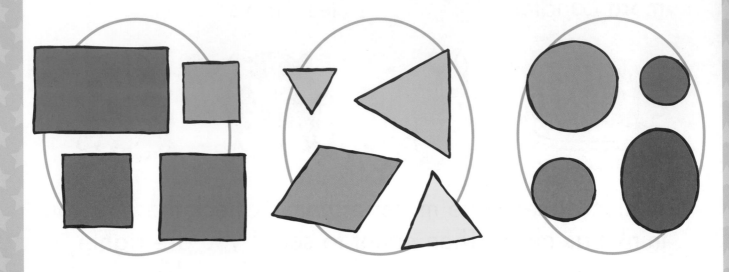

Check all the shapes that are the same in each row.

Note for parent: Recognizing common shapes is a key part of math teaching for your child at this age.

Connect each set of shapes to its name.

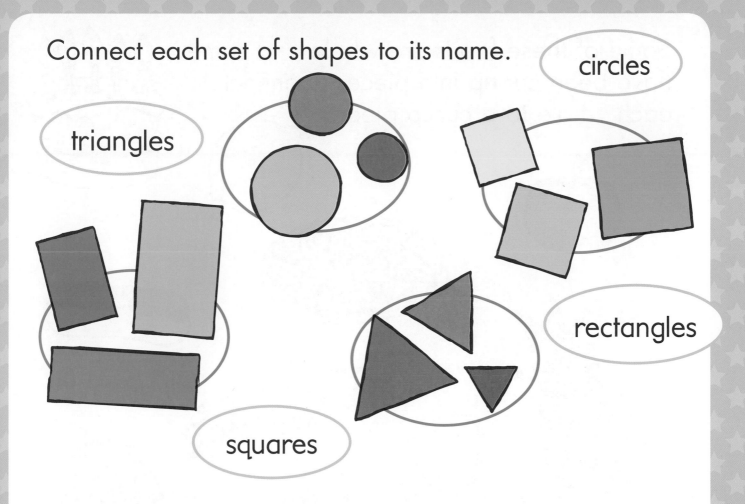

circles

triangles

rectangles

squares

Draw a line to connect the shapes that match.

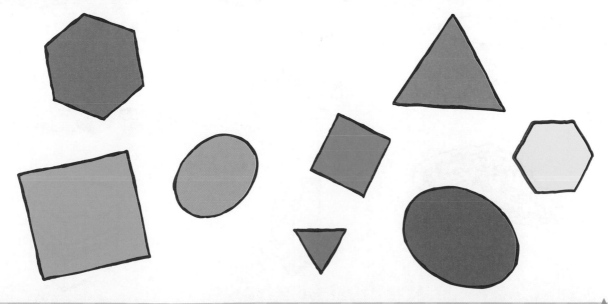

Note for parent: Your child should gradually learn the names of common shapes.

299

Looking at Shapes

Some of these foods are whole and some have been cut up into pieces. Connect each whole to a cut-up piece.

Note for parent: This activity encourages your child to examine shapes closely. Ask your child if they can group the items by a different criteria—like sweet or savory, fruit or vegetable.

Matching Shapes

Color the matching shapes.

 color red

 color green

 color blue

 color orange

Note for parent: This activity gives further practice in examining shapes closely.

301

Solid Shapes

Connect each set of shapes to its name.

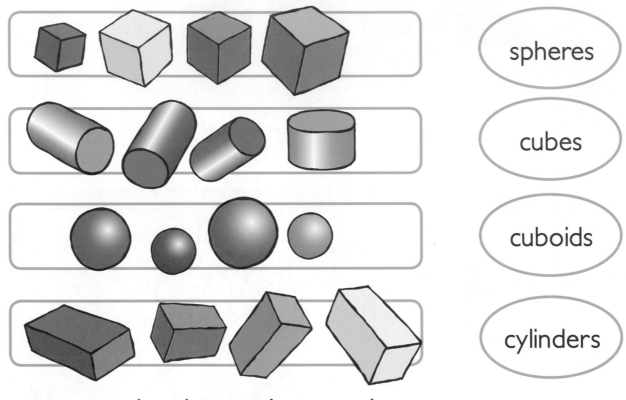

spheres

cubes

cuboids

cylinders

Connect the shapes that match.

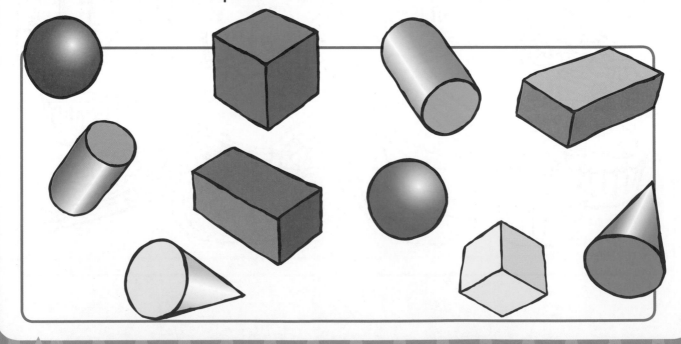

Note for parent: Ask your child to find examples of these solid shapes around the home.
Ask them to recall the shape names as they become familiar to your child.

Quick Quiz

Connect each START food to the correct FINISH food.

 START

add on 0

 add on 3

 add on 6

 add on 6

 FINISH

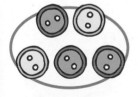 START

take away 3

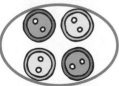 take away 2

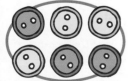 take away 0

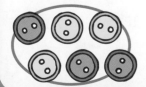 take away 5

Connect each START group to the correct FINISH group.

 FINISH

Note for parent: This activity helps your child to remember about adding and taking away.

303

All about Halves

Color half of each shape.

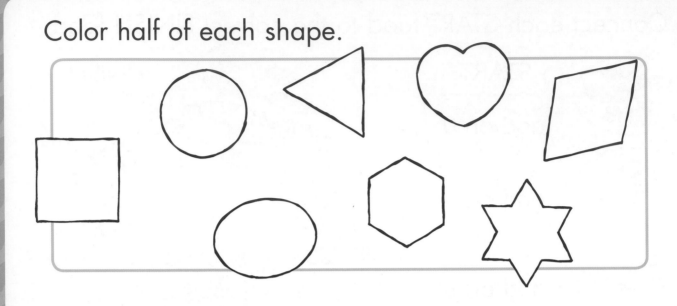

Draw the missing half of each shape.
Connect the complete shape to its name.

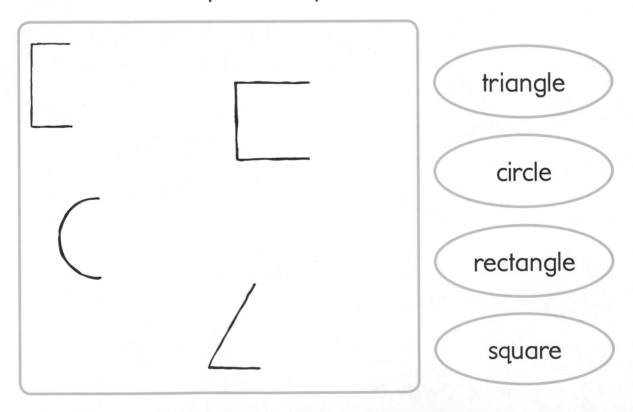

triangle

circle

rectangle

square

Note for parent: Learning about half and equal shares is important in math.

Color half of the items in each container.

Some marbles are put into two bags.
Put a check (✔) if the sharing is equal.
Put a cross (✘) if the sharing is not equal.

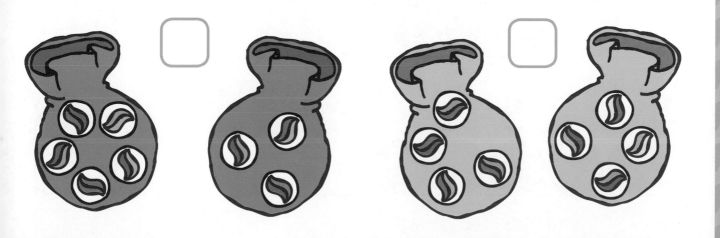

Note for parent: Encourage your child to practice sharing real-life objects equally. Sweets and coins of the same value are good examples to use.

305

Doubles

Double the number of circles in each row.
Write down the new totals.

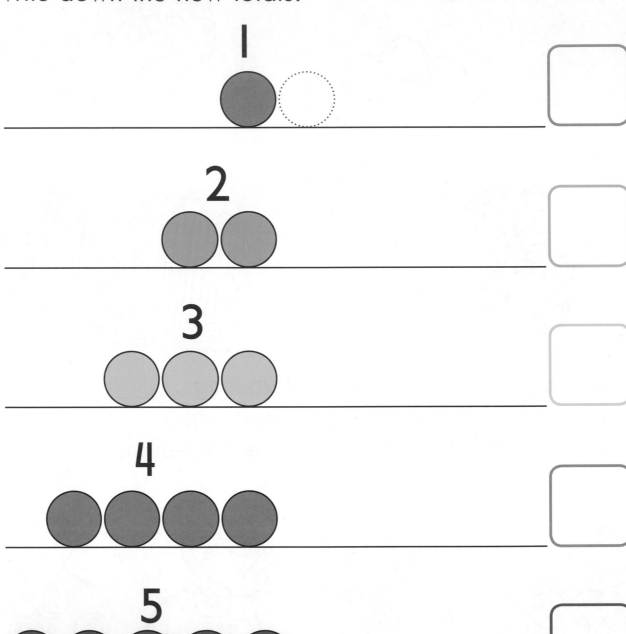

Note for parent: Use the vocabulary twice as many and the same again to explain the meaning of doubling.

Full, Empty, or Half Full?

Some of these bottles and jars are full.
Some are empty. Some are half full.
Draw lines to the right labels.

full   empty   half full

More Doubles

Copy the dots in the boxes to make doubles. Count how many dots all together. Write the answers in the boxes.

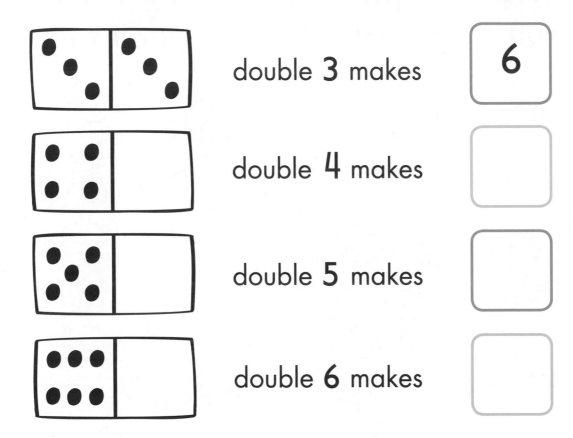

double **3** makes **6**

double **4** makes

double **5** makes

double **6** makes

Add balloons to double the number that each clown holds.

Note for parent: This activity gives practice in understanding doubles.

Halves

Color half of the spots on each ladybug.

Share the pizza equally between the two children.
Draw a line to cut the pizza in half.

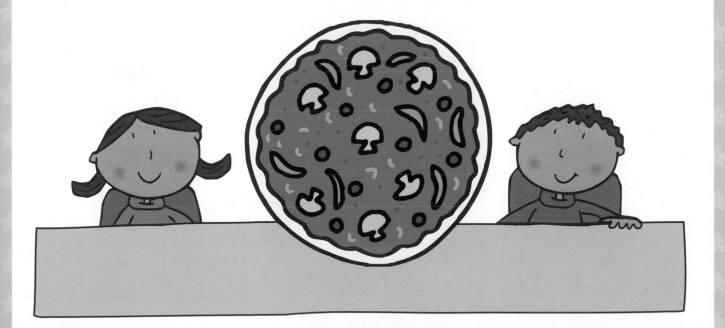

Answers

Phonics

Page 70

Page 71

Tiger, toothbrush, tent, train, tie, tractor.
They all start with t.

Page 72

Pig, mouse, pear, duck, penguin, pen, panda.

Rat and duck do not start with p.

Page 73

Bell, butterfly, cake, banana, frog, bathtub, bee.
Frog and cake do not start with b.

Page 74

Dip, dip, dip,
My little ship,
Big cup and saucer,
Bobbing on the water.
Dip, dip, dip,
My little ship!

Page 75

net   pen   nut
bun   ten   sun

Page 76

s for sun and snail,
a for airplane, t for tree,
p for parrot, i for insect

Page 78

n for net,
m for motorbike,
d for duck,
n—nest, nuts, nail;
m—map, monkey, mushroom;
d—dolphin, dog, drum

Page 79

pan and pan are exactly the same.
mat—at,
pin—tin—din—in,
pan—man,
dad—sad—pad

Page 80

bat   cap
pan   can
dad   van
bag   map

Page 81

pet   pot   red   rod
leg   log   net   not
beg   bog   step   stop

Page 82

r-ub,
d-ub,
t-ub

Page 83

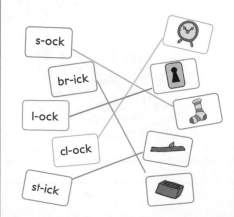

s-ock
br-ick
l-ock
cl-ock
st-ick

Page 85

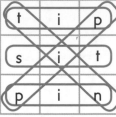

Page 86

pin, bus, log, web, cat, net

Page 87

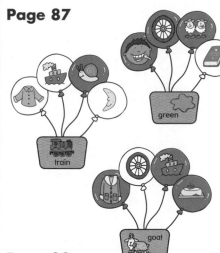

green
train
goat

Page 88

pen—hen; bed—red; net—jet; leg—peg

Page 89

net, red, hen, men, peg, web

Page 90

g—goat, gate; o—orange, owl;
c—car, cup; k—kite, key

Page 91

Kim—it's a name (proper noun).

Page 92

e for egg,
u for umbrella,
r for robot
pen, red, sun, rug, ten, cup, net, nut

Page 93

tick—pick, tack—rack, tuck—duck, rock—tock, peck—deck

Page 94

Hickory, dickory, dock,
The mouse ran up the clock,
The clock struck one,
The mouse was gone,
Hickory, dickory, dock!

Page 95

Peter Piper picked a
peck of pickled peppers!

Where's the peck of pickled
peppers Peter Piper picked?

Page 96

Fred frog likes fresh flies.
Gretel goat likes green grass.
Terrible troll likes tasty toads.
Shane shark likes shiny shrimps.
Harry horse likes harvest hay.

Page 97

sock—clock; black—sack; brick—chick; truck—duck; neck—peck

Page 98

l for leaf, h for horse,
b for bag, f for fox

Page 99

l—ladder, leaf, lion,
h—hat, hen, house,
b—bat, bed, bus,
f—feather, fish, fly

Page 101

hiss   bl-iss   k-iss   m-iss

Pages 102—103

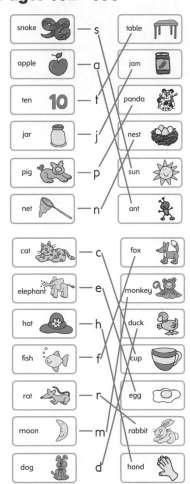

Page 104

Page 105

Page 106

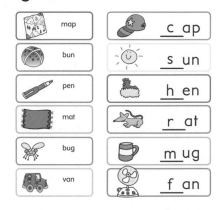

Page 107

Or:
slide, snail, cloud, butterfly, boy

Page 108

h-op—hop, f-ig—fig,
b-it—bit, t-en—ten,
l-ap—lap, m-om—mom

311

Answers

Page 110

pig			
pin			
big			
fin			
bib			
lip			

Page 111
ag—flag, bag
og—dog, frog
ug—mug, rug

Page 112
The doll is not in his suitcase!

Page 113
ten, dog, up, fan, mop, lock

Page 114
Real words—at, on, am, in, up, if

Page 115
Ip is from Inland,
Og is from Onland

Page 116
j for jam, v for vase,
w for watch,
x for x-ray

Page 117
Jack and Jaws,
Raj and Rav,
Tim and Tom,
Pip and Pop,
Vin and Van,
Bex and Bix,
Meg and Mug

Page 118
jog hop pop mop box

Page 119
p̲ot, d̲og, f̲ox, l̲og, m̲o̲p̲, d̲ot

Page 120
y for yo-yo,
z for zebra

Page 121
quiver, quake,
quarrel, quibble,
quick, quack, quiet, quite, quest,
queue

Page 122
at—rat, cat, mat
an—fan, man, can
ap—cap, map

Page 123

Page 124
rug—mug
nut—cut
plum—drum
sun—bun
bull—pull

Page 126

dish			
fish			
bush			
push			
sash			
cash			

Page 127
sh—s̲h̲irt, s̲h̲eep, fis̲h̲
ch—c̲h̲air, c̲h̲eese, c̲h̲erry
th—bat̲h̲tub, pat̲h̲, t̲h̲umb

Page 128
rin̲g̲, si̲n̲k, si̲n̲g, pi̲n̲k, wi̲n̲g, ki̲n̲g

Page 129
su̲n, dol̲l, frog, mo̲m, ba̲t, si̲x, be̲d,
bu̲s

Page 130

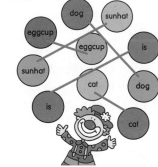

Page 131

mat			
can			
man			
pan			
van			
bat			

Page 132

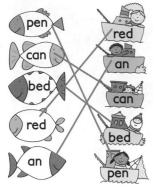

pen	☀	⊘pen	🔑
bed	barrel	ball	bed
pig	pencil	pig	book
red	can	red	kite
ten	dots	tree	ten
web	fish	glove	web

Page 133

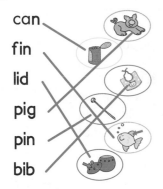

pen, can, bed, red, an

red, an, can, bed, pen

Page 134

can
fin
lid
pig
pin
bib

Page 135
kid, bib, six, lid

Page 136
big—dig; pip—sip; tin—bin;
hid—lid

Page 137
Tim will win the race.
Bob will be last.

Reading and Language Arts

Page 141

b	x	e	s	j	k
e	y	t	p	a	n
d	a	v	n	a	b
z	m	o	m	q	h
c	f	n	l	u	i
a	o	g	p	a	j
t	r	n	e	t	a
d	a	d	w	d	r

Page 142

p b / m n / p d

g k / t c / b d

x n / m k / n m

Page 143
cars, bees, eggs, rugs

Page 144
small, full, new, off

Page 146

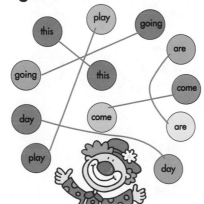

this, play, going, are, going, this, come, day, come, are, play, day

Page 147
cat, pen, fan, dog, mom, dad, pig, cup

Page 148

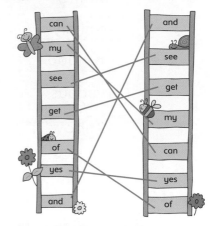

can, my, see, get, of, yes, and

and, see, get, my, can, yes, of

Page 149

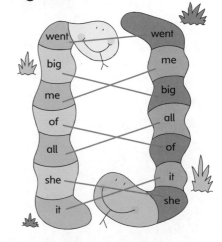

went, big, me, of, all, she, it

went, me, big, all, of, it, she

Page 150

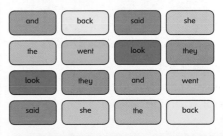

and	back	said	she
the	went	look	they
look	they	and	went
said	she	the	back

A boy (and) a girl (went) to (the) pet shop.
(The) girl (said) she liked (the) puppy.
(They) (went) (back) to (look) at (the) puppy.

Answers

Page 151

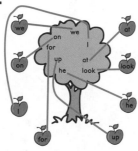

mother
father
grandad
octopus
window
crayon

Page 152

Page 153

Page 154

house, roof, window,
door, garage

Page 155

This is my <u>cat</u>.
It <u>is</u> white.
It has <u>a</u> long tail.
This is a <u>dog</u>.
It <u>can</u> bark.
It is <u>big</u>.

Page 156

The coat is on the back of the
<u>door</u>.
The <u>net</u> is under the bed.
The <u>dinosaur</u> is on the bed.
The chair is near the <u>desk</u>.

Page 157

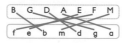 The capitals are:
A, E, J, C, H, F, L,
B, I, K, D, G.

Page 158

Who caught the fish?	Dan	Poppy	(Mia)
Who caught the crab?	(Poppy)	Dan	Ali
What did Dan catch?	(key)	crab	ring

Page 159

boat   goat
coat   foot

moon   boot
spoon   soap

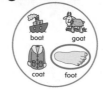
cow   clown
fork   owl

soil   coin
oil   book

Page 160

2   4
1   3

Page 161

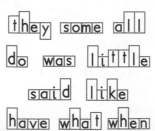

they some all
do was little
said like
have what when

Page 162

1 letter—a, I
2 letters—on, at, up, is, go, we,
   he, am, no
3 letters—for, you, and,
4 letters—like, look, away, said

Page 164

The mouse pulls the <u>cat</u>.
The cat pulls the <u>man</u>.
The <u>man</u> pulls the turnip.

Page 165

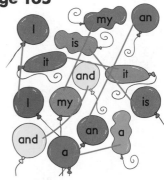

Page 167

I am five.
I am good at reading.
I can read the words
on this page.

Page 168

The dog is in the fog.
The hen is in a pen.
The cat is on a mat.

Page 170

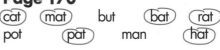

(cat) (mat) but (bat) (rat)
pot (pat) man (hat)

Page 171

ten (tail) tall
maid (mail) mate
rain (nail) name
bell (bail) ball
(trail) fall
wall (snail) snake

314

Page 172

My best friend lives on the <u>moon</u>.
I hope to visit him quite soon.
We'll go for moon walks with his <u>dog</u>,
And float in spacesuits in moon fog.
We'll make chocolate moon bars and crater <u>cakes</u>,
And eat rocket lollies and lunar flakes.
But best of all for having fun,
We'll play hide-and-seek with the <u>sun</u>.

Page 173

The best friend lives on the moon.
They will go for moon walks with his dog.
They will play hide-and-seek with the sun.

Page 177

To the top of the hill

Page 179

cats and dogs,
bats and balls,
pots and pans,
cups and mugs,
hens and eggs

Page 182

night, fright, light, bright, tight, sight, lightning, frightening, fight, alright

Counting

Page 186

Page 187

Page 189

0 → 1 → 2
1 → 2 → 3
2 → 3 → 4
3 → 4 → 5

Page 191

8 (ducklings), 1 (horse),
10 (flowers), 9 (bees), 4 (trees),
5 (pigs), 7 (sunflowers), 2 (cows),
3 (wheels), 6 (sheep)

Page 192

10 carrots

Page 193

6 → 7 → 8
7 → 8 → 9
8 → 9 → 10

Page 194

Page 195

There should be more spaceships colored red than blue in each box.
9 spaceships all together, 10 spaceships all together.

Page 198

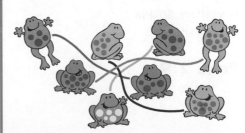

Page 199

3 cows
6 sheep
0 lions
1 dog
2 chickens
0 zebras

Page 200

1 → 2 → 3
2 → 3 → 4
5 → 6 → 7
7 → 8 → 9

Page 201

4 → 3 → 2
5 → 4 → 3
8 → 7 → 6
10 → 9 → 8

Page 202

8 spots, 10 spots, 6 spots, 9 spots, 7 spots, 4 spots.

Answers

Page 203

Clockwise from left:
10 + 0 = 10 spots,
7 + 3 = 10 spots,
9 + 1 = 10 spots,
6 + 4 = 10 spots,
5 + 5 = 10 spots,
8 + 2 = 10 spots,
4 + 6 = 10 spots.

Pages 204–205

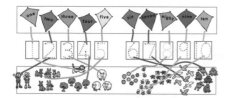

Pages 206–207

6 cookies all together,
6 cakes all together,
5 pizzas all together,
7 ice creams all together,
9 candies all together.
3 and 2 make 5 all together,
4 and 3 make 7 all together,
6 and 2 make 8 all together.

Pages 218

6 green snails
4 yellow snails
5 red snails

Page 219

15 flowers

Pages 220–221

3 drinks
There are enough drinks for 1 each

6 cupcakes
There are enough cupcakes for 2 each

9 balloons
There are enough balloons for 3 each

Page 223

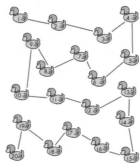

Page 224

6 cookies all together,
6 cakes all together.
6 and 2 make 8 all together.
8 take away 2 leaves 6,
4 take away 2 leaves 2.

Page 225

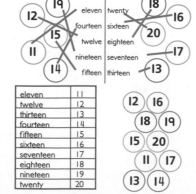

eleven	11
twelve	12
thirteen	13
fourteen	14
fifteen	15
sixteen	16
seventeen	17
eighteen	18
nineteen	19
twenty	20

Page 226

Top train: 9, 10, 11, 12, 13, 14, 15, 16, 17.

Middle train: 11, 12, 13, 14, 15, 16, 17, 18, 19, 20.

Bottom train: 7, 8, 9, 10, 11, 12, 13, 14, 15, 16.
Eleven – 11, fourteen – 14, twelve – 12, fifteen – 15, twenty – 20, sixteen – 16, thirteen – 13, seventeen – 17.

Page 227

Clockwise from top left: rhinoceros, tiger, monkey, elephant.

Math
Page 233

Page 234

3 (cars), 2 (bees), 5 (socks)
4 (spiders)

Page 235

2 (helicopters), 4 (mice),
3 (butterflies), 1 (car)

Page 236

Page 237
more holes; more dogs
Page 238
3 (teddies), 4 (ladybugs)

Page 239
4 (dogs), 2 (ducks)

Page 240
3 kites, 4 bricks, 6 balloons,
7 popsicles

Page 241
3 bananas, 4 bananas
5 bananas, 6 bananas
7 bananas

Page 243
3 take away 1 = 2
5 take away 1 = 4
7 take away 1 = 6
8 take away 1 = 7
Page 244
4 take away 2 = 2
5 take away 2 = 3
8 take away 2 = 6
9 take away 2 = 7

Page 245
Teddy has 7 apples
Robot has 9 apples
Robot has more apples
Tom has 8 oranges
Rob has 9 oranges
Rob has more oranges

Page 246
3 and 2 make 5 all together,
2 and 4 make 6 all together.
Buttons: 1 + 6 = 7;
stars: 4 + 3 = 7;
sweets: 5 + 2 = 7;
hearts: 6 + 3 = 9.
Page 247
3 + 5 = 8, 4 + 4 = 8,
1 + 5 = 6, 2 + 5 = 7.

Page 248
1 + 4 = 5, 3 + 3 = 6,
4 + 6 = 10.
4 + 6 = 10, 8 + 2 = 10.

Page 249
4 + 3 = 7, 2 + 5 = 7, 6 + 2 = 8,
3 + 3 = 6, 6 + 3 = 9, 1 + 5 = 6.
Total of 4: red and yellow scarves;
total of 6: orange and dark blue
scarves;
total of 7: pink and bright blue
scarves;
total of 10: green and purple
scarves.

Page 250
Row 1: 4 take away 2 leaves 2,
6 take away 2 leaves 4,
5 take away 2 leaves 3;
row 2: 8 take away 2 leaves 6,
7 take away 2 leaves 5,
10 take away 2 leaves 8;
row 3: 3 − 2 = 1, 2 − 2 = 0,
9 − 2 = 7.

Page 251

Page 252
4 − 2 = 2, 7 − 3 = 4, 8 − 5 = 3,
5 − 2 = 3, 7 − 4 = 3.

Page 253
4 − 1 = 3, 5 − 3 = 2, 8 − 7 = 1,
5 − 5 = 0, 9 − 5 = 4, 10 − 2 = 8.
10 − 5 and 5 − 0; 8 − 7 and
6 − 5; 10 − 7 and 6 − 3.

Page 254
5 take away 2 leaves 3, 6 take
away 2 leaves 4, 8 take away 2
leaves 6, 4 take away 2 leaves 2,
9 take away 3 leaves 6.

Page 255
5 children, 4 chairs, difference = 1.
7 children, 5 chairs, difference = 2.
6 children, 3 chairs, difference = 3.

Pages 256−257
4 candies add 2 candies =
6 candies, 6 candies add 1 candy
= 7 candies,
5 candies add 3 candies = 8
candies, 7 candies add 2 candies
= 9 candies.
6 drinks take away 1 drink
= 5 drinks,
5 drinks take away 3 drinks
= 2 drinks,
3 drinks take away 2 drinks
= 1 drink,
7 drinks take away 4 drinks
= 3 drinks.

Page 258
line 2: 3 are hidden
line 3: 4 are hidden
line 4: 5 are hidden
line 5: 6 are hidden

Page 259
2 green crayons, 3 pink crayons,
5 crayons all together
4 red crayons, 3 blue crayons,
7 crayons all together
5 yellow crayons, 4 orange
crayons, 9 crayons all together

Answers

Page 260

Page 261

4 (teddy arms), 6 (duck legs), 8 (cat ears)

Page 262

6 − 4 = 2   5 − 4 = 1
8 − 4 = 4   7 − 4 = 3

Page 263

9 − 4 = 5   10 − 4 = 6
4 − 4 = 0

Page 264

2 + 3 = 5,   4 + 4 = 8
5 + 4 = 9

Page 265

5 − 2 = 3,   7 − 4 = 3
10 − 3 = 7

Page 266

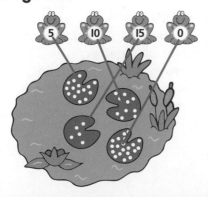

Page 267

Page 268

8 + 3 = 11, 9 + 5 = 14,
8 + 7 = 15, 6 + 7 = 13,
9 + 9 = 18, 6 + 4 = 10.
10 + 3 = 13, 10 + 5 = 15,
10 + 8 = 18, 12 + 6 = 18,
10 + 10 = 20, 15 + 1 = 16.

Page 269

12 − 8 = 4, 12 − 6 = 6,
13 − 4 = 9,
11 − 9 = 2, 16 − 8 = 8,
12 − 5 = 7.
20 − 4 = 16, 20 − 5 = 15,
20 − 6 = 14, 20 − 8 = 12,
20 − 2 = 18, 20 − 7 = 13.

Pages 270-271

2 + 3 = 5, 3 + 4 = 7, 4 + 5 = 9.
3 + 5 = 8 all together,
4 + 2 = 6 all together.
3 + 2 = 5, 2 + 2 = 4,
4 + 3 = 7, 5 + 1 = 6,
6 + 3 = 9, 4 + 5 = 9.

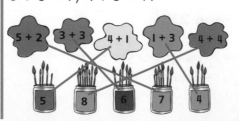

Pages 272–273

7 − 2 = 5, 5 − 2 = 3, 8 − 2 = 6.

Parents need to check child's answer for the last sum on page 18.

5 balls take away 3 balls = 2 balls,

4 balls take away 2 balls = 2 balls,

8 balls take away 4 balls = 4 balls.

Pages 274–275

4 + 2 = 6, 5 + 4 = 9,
7 + 3 = 10,
11 + 2 = 13, 14 + 5 =19,
13 + 7 = 20.
5 + 2 = 7, 4 + 1 = 5, 3 + 3 = 6,
6 + 3 = 9, 3 + 1 = 4.

The missing numbers are:
blue rocket – 6, 9, 10;
green rocket – 1, 3, 4, 8;
red rocket – 8, 9, 12, 15.

Pages 276

6 − 3 = 3, 5 − 2 = 3, 8 − 4 = 4,
13 − 1 = 12, 16 − 3 = 13,
17 − 6 = 11.

Pages 277

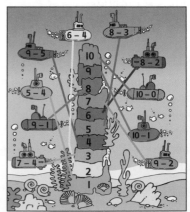

Page 278

2: 0 + 2, 1 + 1, 2 + 0.
3: 1 + 2, 2 + 1, 3 + 0.
4: 1 + 3, 2 + 2, 3 + 1.
5: 1 + 4, 2 + 3, 3 + 2.

Page 279

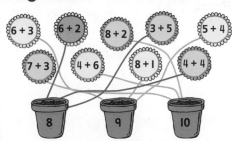

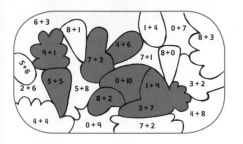

Page 280

1: 2 – 1, 3 – 2, 4 – 3,
5 – 4, 10 – 9.

2: 5 – 3, 4 – 2, 3 – 1,
2 – 0, 10 – 8.

Possible answers include:
6 – 1, 7 – 2, 8 – 3, 9 – 4

Page 281

5 + 2 = 7, 4 + 1 = 5,
4 + 4 = 8.

5 balls take away 3 balls
= 2 balls,

4 balls take away 3 balls
= 1 ball.

Pages 282–283

4 + 3 = 7, 6 + 2 = 8,
5 + 5 = 10, 9 + 1 = 10,
7 + 2 = 9, 3 + 5 = 8,
2 + 4 = 6, 4 + 4 = 8,
6 + 3 = 9.

Missing numbers:

row 1: 6, 8;

row 2: 10, 9, 8, 10.

2 + 2 = 4, 3 + 3 = 6,
4 + 4 = 8, 5 + 5 = 10,
2 + 8 = 10, 6 + 4 = 10,
3 + 7 = 10, 1 + 9 = 10,
10 + 0 = 10.

Missing totals:

green train: 6, 9;

purple train: 3, 6, 8;

red train: 3, 4, 7.

Pages 284–285

6 – 4 = 2, 7 – 3 = 4, 5 – 1 = 4,
8 – 5 = 3, 6 – 3 = 3, 9 – 4 = 5,
10 – 5 = 5, 7 – 4 = 3, 8 – 3 = 5.

The number 4 is hidden in the
grid.

10 – 5 = 5, 8 – 4 = 4, 6 – 3 = 3,
4 – 2 = 2, 10 – 6 = 4, 10 – 2 = 8,
10 – 3 = 7, 10 – 8 = 2, 10 – 9 = 1.

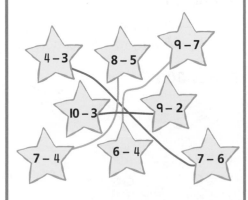

Page 286

total = 4   total = 6

total = 8   total = 10

Page 287

What time is it?
It is 4 o'clock.

It is 3 o'clock. It is 6 o'clock. It is 2 o'clock.

It is 8 o'clock. It is 10 o'clock. It is 12 o'clock.

Page 288

11 o'clock, 8 o'clock, 5 o'clock.

Page 289

From left to right: half past 4,
half-past 10, half-past 7.

Page 290

Answers

Page 291

2 + 4 = 6, 3 + 3 = 6, 5 + 4 = 9,
6 + 4 = 10, 5 + 5 = 10, 2 + 3 = 5,
1 + 7 = 8, 2 + 7 = 9, 2 + 2 = 4.

10 − 1 = 9, 5 − 3 = 2, 4 − 2 = 2,
8 − 3 = 5, 7 − 4 = 3, 6 − 5 = 1,
10 − 6 = 4, 9 − 6 = 3, 7 − 2 = 5.

Pages 292-293

Pages 294

The longest pencil is purple.
The shortest pencil is red.

Pages 295

Pages 296

Pages 297

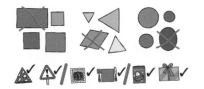

Pages 298

Pages 299

Rectangles, triangles, circles, squares.

Pages 300

Pages 302

Row 1—cubes, row 2—cylinders,
row 3—spheres, row 4—cuboids.

Pages 303

Pages 304

△ triangle, ○ circle,
▭ rectangle, ☐ square.

Page 305

Red bags = ✗; yellow bags = ✔.

Page 306

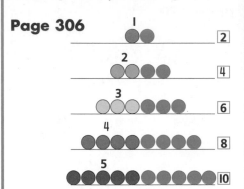

Page 307

full   empty   half-full

Page 308

Double 4 makes 8
Double 5 makes 10
Double 6 makes 12

Page 309

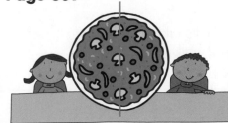